Giver of All Good

Giver of All Good

God as the Beginning and End of Ethics

Chase R. Kuhn

BakerBooks
a division of Baker Publishing Group
Grand Rapids, Michigan

Published by Baker Books
a division of Baker Publishing Group
Grand Rapids, Michigan
BakerBooks.com

Printed in the United States of America

Library of Congress Cataloging-in-Publication Data
Names: Kuhn, Chase R., author
Title: Giver of all good : God as the beginning and end of ethics / Chase R. Kuhn.
Description: Grand Rapids, Michigan : Baker Books, a division of Baker Publishing Group, [2026] | Includes bibliographical references and index.
Identifiers: LCCN 2026008119 | ISBN 9781540906076 paperback | ISBN 9781493465460 ebook
Subjects: LCSH: Christian ethics | Christian life
Classification: LCC BJ1251 .K84 2026
LC record available at https://lccn.loc.gov/2026008119

Cover photograph: 4X5 Coll-Burkatovski Coll. / SuperStock
Cover design by Sarah Gordon

Baker Publishing Group publications use paper produced from sustainable forestry practices and postconsumer waste whenever possible.

26 27 28 29 30 31 32 7 6 5 4 3 2 1

For my children,
Olive, Ezra, Penelope, and Marigold:
May you always know and trust that the Lord is good.

Whoever is wise, let him understand these things;
whoever is discerning, let him know them;
for the ways of the LORD are right,
and the upright walk in them,
but transgressors stumble in them.
Hosea 14:9

Contents

Abbreviations

ANF	*The Ante-Nicene Fathers*. Edited by Alexander Roberts and James Donaldson. 1885–1887. 10 vols. Repr., Hendrickson, 1994.
BDAG	F. W. Danker, W. F. Arndt, and F. W. Gingrich, *Greek-English Lexicon of the New Testament and Other Early Christian Literature*. 3rd ed. University of Chicago Press, 2000 (Bauer-Danker-Arndt-Gingrich).
BECNT	Baker Exegetical Commentary on the New Testament
BTCB	Brazos Theological Commentary on the Bible
CD	*Church Dogmatics*
DBW	Dietrich Bonhoeffer Works
IVP NTCS	IVP New Testament Commentary Series
LW	*Luther's Works*
NPNF[1]	*Nicene and Post-Nicene Fathers*, Series 1. Edited by Philip Schaff. 1886–1889. 14 vols. Repr., Hendrickson, 1994.
NPNF[2]	*Nicene and Post-Nicene Fathers*, Series 2. Edited by Philip Schaff and Henry Wace. 1890–1900. 14 vols. Repr., Hendrickson, 1994.
ZECNT	Zondervan Exegetical Commentary on the New Testament

This thing is good and that good, but take away this and that, and regard good itself if thou canst; so wilt thou see God, not good by a good that is other than Himself, but the good of all good.

Saint Augustine

Lord of all power and might, who art the author and giver of all good things: Graft in our hearts the love of thy name, increase in us true religion, nourish us with all goodness, and of thy great mercy keep us in the same; through Jesus Christ our Lord. *Amen.*

Book of Common Prayer (1662), Collect for
the Seventh Sunday After Trinity

Introduction

The Truth About Morality

All ethical reflection . . . has the goal that I be good, and that the world—by my action—becomes good. If it turns out, however, that these realities, myself and the world, are themselves embedded in a wholly other ultimate reality, namely, the reality of God the Creator, Reconciler, and Redeemer, then the ethical problem takes on a whole new aspect. Of particular importance, then, is not that I become good, or that the condition of the world be improved by my efforts, but that the reality of God show itself everywhere to be the ultimate reality. Where God is known by faith to be the ultimate reality, the source of my ethical concern will be that God be known as the good [das Gute], even at the risk that I and the world are revealed as not good, but as bad through and through. All things appear as in a distorted mirror if they are not seen and recognized in God.[1]

Dietrich Bonhoeffer

My wife and I saw the musical *Wicked* a few years ago. The basic plot of the production questions what we have long called "wicked." The "Wicked Witch" has been on the wrong side of

1. Dietrich Bonhoeffer, *Ethics*, vol. 6 of DBW, ed. Clifford J. Green, trans. Reinhard Krauss et al. (Fortress, 2005), 48.

public opinion, which has been skewed by powers that prefer pretty and conventional over alternative and green. So, the production leads the audience to ask, "Why do we believe what we believe about what is right and wrong? Have the conventional power structures of society misled our beliefs about morality?"

The questions raised in the musical are very contemporary. Regularly, media outlets aim to persuade us that we've been wrong about much of what we've called "bad." In fact, we're told, the "wicked" deserve a fair chance. We must give an equal opportunity to all preferences, opinions, and lifestyles. Moral claims are no longer valid unless the claims are to universal rights and protections. Of course, not all of this has been bad, as there have been many necessary developments in our societal values. But we must not be fooled that all of this is good, either. The frank truth is that we, as a society, no longer have stable moral foundations.[2] How did this change take place?

Our Moral Problem

The most common problem identified in contemporary moral dialogue is the loss of metaphysics. This was most prominently posited by philosopher Alasdair MacIntyre, who blamed the current situation on the Enlightenment's pursuit of knowledge strictly in naturalistic and/or rationalistic terms.[3] This pursuit, he believes, was detrimental to

2. I recognize that "society" is a very broad notion. I am conflicted about where I properly belong. I was raised and theologically trained in the United States of America. I am a resident in Australia, where I've been ministering for more than a decade. And I wrote this chapter in the United Kingdom. My identification of "society" fits each of these Western contexts, as they each, while by no means being the same, have embraced or found themselves in this cultural phenomenon of moral uncertainty.

3. Alasdair MacIntyre, *After Virtue: A Study in Moral Theory*, 3rd ed. (University of Notre Dame Press, 2007). Kant epitomized this modernist position in his search for the categorical imperative: morality rooted in rationality. See Immanuel Kant, *Groundwork of the Metaphysics of Morals*, rev. ed., trans. and ed. Mary Gregor and Jens Timmermann (Cambridge University Press, 2012).

stable morality, as reason cannot provide a secure foundation.[4] What must be retrieved, he argues, are the virtues connected to metaphysics. Others have noted that modernity's failure to provide a stable moral foundation left postmoderns with nothing but the self to turn to. Today, self-expression has become the most virtuous thing.[5] This "true to self" ethic is indicative of the relativism of postmodern morality.

Theologian Carl Trueman has engaged this moral conundrum, particularly in modern sexual ethics. Following MacIntyre and sociologist Philip Rieff, Trueman also notes that the lack of a metaphysical foundation has led to moral volatility. Contemporary morality is doomed to a constant state of flux, having produced morals that are here today and gone tomorrow. If you seek moral approval today, you may be damned tomorrow. As an example, Trueman says that "the term 'mistress' has become too flattering a metaphor for moral relevance, implying as it does a degree of longevity in the relationship. Today, moral tastes have too short a shelf life for that. Indeed, embracing the moral spirit of the age is now more akin to having a one-night stand—and that with somebody who kicks you out of bed in the morning and calls the police."[6]

4. Modernist epistemology similarly struggled in this way of relating the noumenal and phenomenal. For a helpful Christian response to this epistemological problem, see Herman Bavinck, *Christian Worldview*, ed. and trans. Nathaniel Gray Sutanto et al. (Crossway, 2019). Bavinck demonstrates that a theological vision of the world is necessary to know the coherence between subject and object. "This confession [God the Father, the Almighty, Creator of heaven and earth] is not only the first article of our Christian faith, but also the foundation and cornerstone of all knowledge and science. Only with this confession can one understand and uphold the harmony of subject and object, of thinking and being. The organs of our perception are thus connected to the elements, out of which the whole cosmos is composed, by virtue of a common origin, and so each of us knows the world in a particular way and from a particular side" (38–39).

5. See Charles Taylor, *The Ethics of Authenticity* (Harvard University Press, 1992). See also Glynn Harrison, *A Better Story: God, Sex and Human Flourishing* (Inter-Varsity, 2017).

6. Carl R. Trueman, "The Strange Fate of *Hamilton* and *Harry Potter*," *First Things*, January 6, 2022, https://www.firstthings.com/web-exclusives/2022/01/the-strange-fate-of-hamilton-and-harry-potter.

In political debates and media reports, moral confusion is exacerbated by arguments used to influence the masses. Christians living in this environment feel the problem acutely. Christian discipleship insists on a lifestyle that rejects conformity to the world and instead pursues discernment of the will of God (Rom. 12:1–2). Knowing this will is a spiritual pursuit that the Holy Spirit energizes us for as we encounter Scripture's authoritative account of reality. But confusion abounds about how the authority of God's Word reaches everyday scenarios, let alone major political debates. Furthermore, Christians today have been led to question whether the Bible's teaching on morality is oppressive—a means of some keeping power over others. Much better, society contends, is to let authenticity abound, where one's experience frames one's moral direction.

But even experience as a basis for morality can be complicated. Friedrich Nietzsche says morality is something governed by our experience, especially our socioeconomic background. Thus, he divides morality into master moralities and slave moralities.[7] He argues that the will to power dominates all human beings, even equating this with life itself.[8] For the nobility ("master moralities"), it is the power within oneself and over oneself. The responsibility of the nobility is to themselves and their kind. For those who are oppressed ("slave moralities"), power over their oppressor is valued; this may manifest itself in achieving power over the consequences wrought by the oppressor, bringing relief to those oppressed. Within the experience of people and the ensuant morality they identify with, there are naturally formed herds. These herds, Nietzsche believes, reinforce the values of the moral sets.[9] He argues that each human being is born with an innate instinct to obey. This obedience seeks a commander, and within a community, voices

7. Friedrich Nietzsche, *Beyond Good and Evil*, trans. Marion Faber (Oxford University Press, 1998), 153, 260.

8. Nietzsche, *Beyond Good and Evil*, 152–53, 259.

9. Nietzsche, *Beyond Good and Evil*, 87, 201.

arise to command a herd. Belonging often comes with obedience. But the commanders cannot lead from their own initiative, so they instead fool themselves into believing they are under higher orders—the command of another. The religious are under "god." Nietzsche contends that religion amounts to the abandonment of rationality: "Christianity has been the most disastrous form of human presumptions yet. . . . They have bred a diminished, almost ludicrous species, a herd animal, something good-natured, sickly, mediocre, today's European."[10]

The onslaught of progressive ideology in Western culture—not new but intensified and increasingly hostile in the Information Age—has left many Christians uneasy. Some dream of a better day, a golden age of the past, when their beliefs were more societally acceptable. In fact, traditional Christian values are increasingly shunned not only as old-fashioned but as hateful and ultimately detrimental to society. So, Christians feel pressure either to capitulate to the spirit of the age or to hide their moral beliefs, treating them as a private code of conduct. How are we to live in the face of such challenges to moral thinking in our context? Can we still say that God is good? Are his ways *still* good for us now?

Theology and Ethics

My goal in this book is to inspire confidence in the moral vision of the Bible. I will argue that there is a moral order that is real, determined by God, and relevant to all human beings.[11] Goodness comes to us from God himself; our world was made with a good order that emanates from God's own goodness. In fact, creation only knows the "good life" when it is properly aligned with God. What follows is a theological

10. Nietzsche, *Beyond Good and Evil*, 57, 62.

11. While animals and other creatures are part of the created order, moral agency is reserved for human beings who are uniquely accountable to God. There appears to be moral agency for angels as well, but that is beyond the scope of this book.

framework of morality, exploring the objectivity of the moral order in accordance with the God who has made the world and sovereignly rules over it. In my exploration of this objective order, I will also account for our subjective experience of the world as fallen human beings, naming the challenges we face related to knowledge, authority, and decision-making in a world fraught with tension as all creation groans in awaiting redemption (Rom. 8:19–25). By the end of the book, I hope readers will proceed with greater confidence in their daily moral deliberations.

As a theologian, naturally I have reflected on ethics as it relates to doctrine. In one sense, this is because my discipline trained me to think from first principles. But often ethicists dive headlong into addressing issues without specifying a rationale for their deliberative process. And where metaethics—the subset of ethics concerned with the nature of goodness and the knowledge thereof—is addressed, too often it is in a highly descriptive fashion. Through my years of teaching ethics and engaging with ethics textbooks, I have become more and more convinced that theology sits as the foundation of morality. Our ethics need a theological orientation for us to know good and evil and discern right and wrong. Furthermore, doctrine is not for abstract thought but for living and relating, so ethics is a necessary complement to theology.[12]

In the Bible, the link between doctrine and ethics is presented most clearly in the Pastoral Epistles. In Paul's First Letter to Timothy,

12. There is a long discussion about the relationship between theology and ethics, and I cannot explore the nuances of the voices in the discussion here. For a few different positions, consider Karl Barth, *Ethics*, ed. Dietrich Braun, trans. Geoffrey W. Bromiley (Wipf & Stock, 1981), 1–20, where Barth contends that theological ethics *is* dogmatics. Alternatively, Oliver O'Donovan believes that ethical questions are not the same as dogmatic questions; see O'Donovan, "What Can Ethics Know About God?" in *The Doctrine of God and Theological Ethics*, ed. Alan J. Torrance and Michael Banner (T&T Clark, 2006), 33–46. According to O'Donovan, to say ethics is dogmatics is "high-handed." Finally, Stanley Hauerwas contends that ethics is the starting point of theological reflection, and that we should *not* begin with theological convictions only then to discern necessary practical responses; see Hauerwas, *The Peaceable Kingdom: A Primer in Christian Ethics*, 2nd ed. (SCM, 2003), 16.

he outlines the challenges that have arisen in Ephesus because some have taught false doctrine and swerved from the truth, teaching without understanding (1:4–7). Paul encourages Timothy to remain in Ephesus so that he might defend the faith (1:3). Paul then clarifies something about doctrine and morality:

> Now we know that the law is good, if one uses it lawfully, understanding this, that the law is not laid down for the just but for the lawless and disobedient, for the ungodly and sinners, for the unholy and profane, for those who strike their fathers and mothers, for murderers, the sexually immoral, men who practice homosexuality, enslavers, liars, perjurers, and *whatever else is contrary to sound doctrine, in accordance with the gospel of the glory of the blessed God* with which I have been entrusted. (1 Tim. 1:8–11, emphasis added)

Paul says there is an inextricable link between sound doctrine and morality. In other words, true morality accords with sound doctrine. The gospel of God leads people in a moral way of life. To put it negatively, immorality springs from false ("unhealthy") doctrine.

Given this connection between theology and ethics, this book will demonstrate the significance of core doctrinal convictions for an ethical framework. Chapters are organized according to key theological categories, but I deliberately address topics in view of their moral significance. This is not to say that anthropological concerns are primary—quite the contrary. I am framing moral concerns in a way that places *theology* first. God sets the agenda, and all matters are considered relative to his concerns for his creation.

An Outline of the Theological Frame of Ethics

The first chapter shows Jesus as the centerpiece of our moral discovery. If we are ever to understand morality properly, it will be as we know Jesus. Jesus is the first and last, for it is by him and for him that all things exist (Rev. 1:17; Col. 1:16). The chapter builds on Jesus's claim to be the Way, the Truth, and the Life: (1) the Way: the hypostatic union; (2) the Truth: the preeminence of the Son; and (3) the Life: the eschatological Man. I argue that Jesus Christ provides an ontological and teleological orientation to ethics, as he reveals true humanity and divinity.

The second chapter proposes retrieving God's goodness as the foundation of moral reality. Historically, I focus on Augustine and Aquinas, with some interaction with the Reformed Orthodox theologians after them. I give attention to the correlation between the divine essence, will, and works. I consider the divine essence *in se* (internally) before turning to the divine works *ad extra* (externally). The fundamental difference between uncreated and created beings is shown not to discount moral reality but instead serves as the foundation of it. The conclusion of the chapter is that God's essence guarantees the goodness of the creation and serves as the ultimate reference point for morality.

The third chapter builds on the conclusion of the preceding chapter. Because God is good, the creation he makes is good. Creation is a free act of God in love, asymmetrical in dependency; the Creator is free and unconstrained, the creation ever sustained by the Creator. This relationship is displayed in the fundamental order God bestowed on the cosmos. We can observe this order as a hierarchical structure, seen in both generic and telic kinds. Eschewing this metaphysical account leads to an arbitrary system(s) of valuation.

The fourth chapter considers the result of denying divine order. I consider moral choice and human freedom, examining human agency in the garden of Eden and the ramifications of that choice on the rest of the created order. The great challenge to morality has always been *faith*—do we trust that God is good and that his ways are right? Faith is the great difficulty of our subjective experience. Juxtaposing the life of faith with self-determination, I consider the consequences of sin: a creation groaning, the curse, and a disordered cosmos. Ultimately, regeneration liberates sinners from their perpetual failure to apprehend true value and restores God's order and orientation to life.

The fifth chapter examines life after the fall. Redemption constitutes a certain restoration of dignity. Indeed, Christ himself dignifies humanity. But is human participation in the created order devoid of good apart from redemption? This chapter seeks a theological locus for human dignity that accounts for the goodness of life for all humans, even after Eden. Questions surface about the *imago Dei* and the feasibility of ultimate and penultimate ends for humanity. Here, I engage recent discussions of "two kingdoms theology" and its rejoinders. I will argue that, though postlapsarian humanity is depraved, God allows preservation of particular "good(s)" for the perpetuation of society, for the sake of the elect, and ultimately in service of a doxological end. The theological locus of dignity is truly theological; God, the Creator, graciously provides for human beings in both common and particular ways.

In the sixth chapter, we will consider how the challenge of faith is now complicated by the noetic effects of the fall. In our desire as humans to *decide* right and wrong, we have been cursed to not know right from wrong in an ultimate sense. Though the curse is pervasive, we are not without God's gracious provision. Following the Thomistic four laws (eternal, divine, natural, and human) and their reception amongst the Reformed Orthodox, I examine what can be known about morality and by whom. Building on a rich tradition, I explore how two kingdoms theology aligns with this moral knowledge and provides a model for political participation, which I elaborate on later.

Chapter seven examines the implications of the theology explored in the opening chapters. Putting theology first, we recognize morality as something received rather than constructed in our moral consideration. I contrast a wide range of proposals for singular modes of ethics (e.g., virtue, utilitarian) with the Bible's presentation of morality, which I argue is multimodal. Unity in biblical morality is not in a singular mode but in the theological, moral vision. I demonstrate this unity in diversity through a worked example. The chapter concludes with a brief proposal on how biblical modes of reasoning impact moral deliberation.

In the eighth chapter, I explain how morality is not simply an individual concern. One of God's purposes for the church is the moral formation of his people. As the people of God are drawn together with other believers in Christ, they are changed into the likeness of Christ *together*. The church provides the space for morality to be tested and for transformation to be graciously and patiently cultivated. I begin by looking once more at the problems that combat the formation of a community, then the nature of what is involved in a community and how the gospel enables a genuine community to form. The church's purpose at the core is knowing and showing forth the love of God in Christ, according to the newness of life in the Spirit. As Christians live together in fellowship, we are together being prepared as a beautiful bride in anticipation of the return of Christ, the bridegroom.

In the final chapter, I briefly consider the hope of the Christian life. Every Christian has the promise of the Holy Spirit perfecting the work of Christ in them. God has given us "all things that pertain to life and godliness" (2 Pet. 1:3). What does it mean for Christians to live in the knowledge of Christ, in the expectation of his coming? Essential to this question is the matter of public presence. What should Christians hope for in the broader culture? Returning to two kingdoms theology, we find a realistic expectation for cultural participation, grounded in christological hope. I encourage us to live in faith with eschatological expectation, as the promised coming of Christ reveals the true end of all creation.

1

Jesus Christ

The Beginning and End of Morality

To speak of the world without speaking of Christ is pure abstraction. The world stands in relationship to Christ whether the world knows it or not.[1]

Dietrich Bonhoeffer

MY WIFE RECENTLY WROTE AND illustrated a children's book. Our children demonstrated something telling of our human condition in their response to the book's pictures: They immediately sought to identify themselves in the story, and did so as they thought best. The images had no resemblance to our children. Nonetheless, they saw themselves. This is a simple illustration of how each person seeks to find themselves in a narrative—both to know and be known. Each of us thinks about the world from the vantage point of self and the relationships to the self.

1. Dietrich Bonhoeffer, *Ethics*, vol. 6 of DBW, ed. Clifford J. Green, trans. Reinhard Krauss et al. (Fortress, 2005), 68.

The self is where John Calvin began his *Institutes of the Christian Religion*. He did this because our encounter of the world is always first and foremost from the perspective of self. But Calvin was quick to show that true self-knowledge does not come to us until we see ourselves in the light of God: "No one can look upon himself without immediately turning his thoughts to the contemplation of God, in whom he 'lives and moves' (Acts 17:28)."[2] So too with morality.

We constantly consider morality from the perspective of self. We condition morality based on our own experience: our history, our feelings, our aspirations, and so forth. But we do not have the proper orientation to reality until we find ourselves in God. As Dietrich Bonhoeffer states, "The source of a Christian ethic is not the reality of one's own self, not the reality of the world, nor is it the reality of norms and values. It is the reality of God that is revealed in Jesus Christ."[3] But this source of morality in Jesus is not ultimately uninterested in the self; rather, it guides the interpretation of the self. As with Calvin, so too with Bonhoeffer: We can only know goodness for ourselves if we find ourselves participating in the reality of God's goodness manifested in Christ.[4]

In this chapter, I begin to construct a theological framework for morality with Jesus Christ. I start here because he is the eternal Word, who in the beginning was with God and was God (John 1:1). Furthermore, "all things were created through him and for him" (Col. 1:16), and in him "all things hold together" (1:17). In short, Jesus is the disclosure of true reality.[5] To know true goodness is to know the good God who framed reality. We know God in and through the incarnation of the eternal Son—the Word of God—the man Jesus Christ. We will consider three facets of Christology—the hypostatic

2. John Calvin, *Institutes of the Christian Religion*, ed. John T. McNeill, trans. Ford Lewis Battles (Westminster, 1960), 1.1.1–8.

3. Bonhoeffer, *Ethics*, 49.

4. Bonhoeffer, *Ethics*, 49–51.

5. Bonhoeffer, *Ethics*, 50.

union, the preeminence of the Son, and the eschatological Man—in order to situate the theological exploration of morality that will follow in subsequent chapters. I will argue that Jesus Christ provides both ontological and teleological orientation to ethics, since he reveals true humanity and true divinity.

The Way: The Hypostatic Union

The primary purpose of considering the hypostatic union in relation to morality is to recognize in Jesus that we are given both knowledge of and access to moral order. The Council of Chalcedon of AD 451 identified the hypostatic union as the way of holding in tension the two natures of Christ in one person. The resulting definition states that he is "at once complete in Godhead and complete in manhood." These two natures exist in Christ "without confusion, without change, without division, without separation; the distinction of natures being in no way annulled by the union, but rather the characteristics of each nature being preserved and coming together to form one person and subsistence, not as parted or separated into two persons, but one and the same Son and Only-begotten God the Word, Lord Jesus Christ."

Chalcedon sought to articulate in creedal form what is found in the Epistle to the Hebrews (and elsewhere), namely that Jesus is the "radiance of the glory of God and the exact imprint of his nature" (1:3), and that "he had to be made like his brothers in every respect" (2:17), sharing in "flesh and blood" (2:14). This union of the two natures in one person was perfectly enabled through the work of the Holy Spirit.[6] The significance of this hypostatic union for morality is seen in six key ways.

6. For an excellent treatment of this work, see Michael Horton, *Rediscovering the Holy Spirit: God's Perfecting Presence in Creation, Redemption, and Everyday Life* (Zondervan Academic, 2017), 95–104.

The hypostatic union and revelation. First, the Son reveals the Father and, in doing so, reveals the divine will. Jesus expected believers to observe his identity in what has been called both Christology from below and Christology from above.[7] "Below" because Jesus's works testify to him (John 5:36). "Above" because the Scriptures bear witness to him (5:39). Thus, Jesus explained to the disciples, "Whoever has seen me has seen the Father" (14:9), and "I am in the Father and the Father is in me" (14:11). We notice several features of this revelation. First, Jesus demonstrates the works of the Father in his actions. Jesus shows what it is for a man, as a man, to truly live life obediently to the Father. Second, Jesus reveals the Father in accordance with the Scriptures because Jesus is the embodiment of the eternal Word (1:1–2), the eternal Son (Heb. 1:1–2). In Jesus, we have clear communication of divine reality and intention. The Son, who has always been with the Father and in the Father, makes him known—exposing ultimate reality. But he also verifies the divine will for humanity, especially in covenantal terms. God simultaneously demonstrates that he holds humanity to account for sin and that he is faithful to his chosen people, showing them mercy, love, and justice. The significance of these features will become more apparent in the following points.

The hypostatic union and impeccable humanity. Second, the hypostatic union is a demonstration of impeccable humanity. Jesus's life makes concrete the abstractness of God's holiness. That is, God's holiness was always perceived as a transcendent reality in the history of Israel, signified in the separation of Israel from God at Sinai (Exod. 19:10–25; cf. Heb. 12:18–24), and in the cultic worship of the tabernacle/temple by the veil of separation (e.g., Exod. 26:31–35;

7. This should not be confounded with "low" or "high" Christology. See George Hunsinger, "*Salvator Mundi*: Three Types of Christology," in *Christology, Ancient and Modern: Explorations in Constructive Dogmatics*, ed. Oliver D. Crisp and Fred Sanders (Zondervan Academic, 2013), 42–59.

Lev. 16; Heb. 9). But in Christ, the holiness of God is presented in human form. In Jesus's life, this was signified in his moral perfection, namely in his obedience to the Father. God's association with his people called for them to emulate holiness as he is holy (Exod. 19:6; 1 Pet. 1:15). Jesus, as *the* man and preeminent Israelite, lived without sin (Heb. 4:15; 9:14). The implications of his impeccability are manifold, but I note just a few here.

First, we should hold fast our confession of Christ as the Son of God and Son of Man (Heb. 4:14); the hypostatic union is confirmed in the reception of Christ at the right hand of the Father (Heb. 4:14; 6:19; 8:1–2; 10:12–13). Second, Jesus provides an imitable way of life (1 Cor. 11:1; 1 Pet. 2:21). Jesus shows us what it means to live life as a true human being. Third, we should see that Jesus's life was indeed morally pure as confirmed in his reception as the one perfect sacrifice for sin; he "offered himself without blemish to God" (Heb. 9:14). This gives us confidence that the Father received his life on our behalf; the Son's work as our Great High Priest was and remains effective. Because of Jesus's impeccable life, and therefore perfect sacrifice for our sins, we can draw near to the throne of God in confidence for help.

The hypostatic union and atonement. Third, the hypostatic union was required to atone for humanity's sin. Hebrews 2 tells us that the eternal Son took on flesh *for* humanity's redemption. We have just seen that Jesus lived a sinless life and therefore was able to offer himself without blemish as a sacrifice. However, there is congruence with humanity's estate: Jesus came "*in the likeness of sinful flesh* and for sin [*en homoiōmati sarkos hamartias*]" (Rom. 8:3, emphasis added), though he remained sinless in the flesh. This paradoxical condition of assuming "sinful flesh" but being "without sin" is crucial to the offering Jesus made on behalf of humanity's sin. As Gregory Nazianzen explains, "That which he [Jesus] has not assumed he has not healed."[8]

8. Gregory Nazianzen, *Epistles* 101 (*NPNF*[2] 7:440).

If humanity were to be fully redeemed, then Christ would need to be fully human. So, "he had to be made like his brothers in every respect" (Heb. 2:17). Giving further exposition, Gregory writes, "It was that He might destroy the condemnation by sanctifying like by like, then as He needed flesh for the sake of the flesh which had incurred condemnation, and soul for the sake of soul, so, too, He needed mind for the sake of mind, which not only fell in Adam, but was the first to be affected, as the doctors say of illnesses."[9] In taking on our flesh, Jesus was able to overcome our problems. It was in his body that he bore our sins (1 Pet. 2:23). It is by his wounds that we are healed (Isa. 53:5).[10]

The hypostatic union and the justice of God. Fourth, the hypostatic union is a demonstration of the justice of God. In our reckoning of a moral order, we search for a place in history to see good divine action holding evil to account. In offering his only begotten Son, God demonstrated that he could not and would not allow sin to go unpunished. At the cross, Jesus withstood the divine wrath owed to sin. At the cross, Jesus also conquered every evil power (Eph. 1:19–23; Heb. 2:14–15). If we'd like to know how severe the plight of humanity is, we must look no further than the cross, where the Son of Man died for humanity. It should not be lost on us how miserable the consequences of sin are for humanity—death. The result of this justice dealt on our behalf to the Christ is a release from slavery to fear of death (Heb. 2:15). In fact, 1 John 4 makes it plain that "perfect love casts out fear," and fear has to do with judgment. If we know the love of God in Christ, there is no cause for fear, for Jesus has conquered death, having made atonement for us. But we must recognize that

9. Gregory Nazianzen, *Epistles* 101 (*NPNF*^{2} 7:441). For an interesting exposition on the fall of humanity's mind and the redemptive work of Christ, see Thomas F. Torrance, *Atonement: The Person and Work of Christ*, ed. Robert T. Walker (IVP Academic, 2009), 437–47.

10. I originally wrote a portion of this paragraph for a Moore College course on the victory of Christ.

there were two necessary hurdles for our atonement and reconciliation. According to Francis Turretin, "Satisfaction (interposing) removes a twofold obstacle: on the part of God, whose justice must be satisfied; on the part of men, the guilt of whose sin must be expiated by suffering the punishment due to it."[11] So, in the offering of Christ on the cross—the One who is fully God and man—we have the full satisfaction of the justice of God and the full restitution of humanity, as we shall see in the next point.

The hypostatic union and imputation. Fifth, the hypostatic union provides for the imputation of righteousness to humanity. The apostle Paul declares that "in Christ God was reconciling the world to himself, not counting their trespasses against them" (2 Cor. 5:19). He expounds on the means of this reconciliation: "For our sake he made him to be sin who knew no sin, so that in him we might become the righteousness of God" (v. 21). Thus, imputation has two dimensions: what is imputed to Christ and what is imputed to those found in Christ by faith. To Christ is imputed the sin of humanity. This is not active sin on his part, but rather the condemnation of sin in the likeness of sinful flesh. Only as a bona fide man, bearing real flesh, could he carry the condemnation owed to humanity for sin. Thus, he served as our representative in his death. But because of his sinless perfection and the just judgment of God upon Christ, he was raised from the dead. So now those found in Christ by faith are counted as Christ is—righteous. Turretin explains that Christ's substitution was "a true and proper satisfaction made by the payment of a full price and which meritoriously obtains the liberation of the guilty on the ground of justice."[12] "There is therefore now no condemnation for those who are in Christ Jesus" (Rom. 8:1). And there is, therefore, no longer death to die as a consequence of sin. Being found in Christ,

11. Francis Turretin, *Institutes of Elenctic Theology*, 3 vols., trans. George Musgrave Giger, ed. James T. Dennison Jr. (P&R, 1994), 2:14.11.18.

12. Turretin, *Institutes*, 2:14.11.1.

we hold the promise of resurrection based on the righteousness of Christ credited to us.

The hypostatic union and reality. Finally, both the occurrence of the hypostatic union and the preservation of that union through death in resurrection life confirms something of reality. The resurrection of Jesus Christ validates that the hypostatic union took place in the virgin birth.[13] What was veiled in the flesh is now confirmed: "Truly this was the Son of God" (Matt. 27:54). This means that all we have seen of Jesus and what he tells us of morality is validated. As T. F. Torrance writes, "In the risen Christ our human nature in its creaturely and temporal existence is redeemed and renewed and established through being taken up in its affirmed reality into the life of God."[14]

In Jesus, we see that God truly cares for his creation and is willing to engage creation in the most intimate way. God entered into his creation, the Creator becoming Creature, and this union now continues eternally for the sake of humanity. Therefore, in Christ, we see a crucial link between the good order of God's creation and his provision for the redemption and restoration of that good order even through judgment. We turn now to see more of this order revealed in Christ.

The Truth: The Preeminent Son

I have just teased out some of the relevance of the hypostatic union for morality. This was necessary before I could make this second point: Jesus Christ, the Word of God incarnate, reveals to us the world's moral order. That Jesus is none other than the eternal Son provides

13. T. F. Torrance has helpfully referred to the virgin womb and virgin tomb as twin signs of the reality of the hypostatic union. See Thomas F. Torrance, *Incarnation: The Person and Life of Christ*, ed. Robert T. Walker. (IVP Academic, 2008), 96–97.

14. Thomas F. Torrance, *Space, Time and Resurrection* (T&T Clark, 2018), 98.

us with great confidence in the good order God intended for the world, in God's ongoing provision for the world, and in his plans for the judgment and salvation of the world. It is *only* through the Son that we know the Father. Here in this section, we will examine Colossians 1:15–17, observing three things: First, Jesus is the Word before the world; second, Jesus is the One who orders the world; and third, Jesus is the sustainer of the world.

Before considering these points, I want to explore the necessity of Christ for knowing moral order.[15] What is *not* meant by the necessity of Jesus Christ for morality is that there is no morality or moral knowledge for those outside of Christ. Precisely because Christ has ordered the whole world, many observable relations within the created order testify to morality. And because of this ordering and the provision of God within that order even after the fall, humanity can participate in and know the moral order in a penultimate sense. But there is a specific affirmation of this order in the resurrection of Christ from the dead as a man. In the resurrection, Christ said "Amen" to the goodness of the created order.[16] This is akin to the prototype of judgment in the flood narrative of Genesis 6–8, where God destroyed

15. Later, I will give a fuller treatment of epistemology in relation to moral knowledge.
16. Oliver O'Donovan explains this well, avoiding the polarization that so often occurs between general and special revelation:

> Creation and redemption each has its ontological and epistemological aspect. There is the created order and there is natural knowledge; there is the new creation and there is revelation in Christ. This has encouraged a confusion of the ontological and epistemological in much modern theology, so that we are constantly presented with the unacceptably polarized choice between an ethic that is revealed and an ethic that is based on creation and so is naturally known. This polarization deprives redemption and revelation of their proper theological meaning as the divine reaffirmation of created order. If, on the other hand, it is the gospel of the resurrection that assures us of the stability and permanence of the world which God has made, then neither of the polarized options is right. In the sphere of revelation, we will conclude, and only there, can we see the natural order as it really is and overcome the epistemological barriers to an ethic that conforms to nature. This nature involves all men, and indeed . . . does not exclude certain 'natural knowledge' which is also a part of man's created endowment. And yet

the world by a flood but did not begin again *de novo*. The problem was not the materials of the creation but rather humanity's disobedience to the order God had set for his creation.

In Christ, we have the demonstration of an ordered life and provision for a return to order, or the *reordering* of the world. Without Christ, humanity can participate in the created order such that they still see "good" in the world *penultimately*. But with Christ, humanity is given access to participate in *ultimate* goodness, even the divine life and the kingdom of heaven. I will explore these themes in greater detail in the final chapter, but for now, we consider three points related to how Christ orders creation.

The Word before the world. First, Jesus is the Word that was before the world. Here notice again what was mentioned above: In Jesus Christ, we see the eternal Son of God, the Second Person of the triune Godhead. The significance of this identification should not be missed. In Jesus, we are given the revelation of ultimate reality, the Alpha and Omega, the One "who is and who was and who is to come, the Almighty" (Rev. 1:8). He is indeed the "image of the invisible God, the firstborn of all creation" (Col. 1:15). Of this revelation, Bonhoeffer explains, "The ultimate, or final, reality discloses itself to be at the same time the first reality, God as the first and last, the Alpha and Omega. . . . For what meaning would the goodness of human beings and the world have without God? Since God, however, as ultimate reality is no other than the self-announcing, self-witnessing, self-revealing God in Jesus Christ, the question of good can only find its answer in Jesus Christ."[17] Good has a reference and a source, and in Jesus Christ, we are shown this source: the eternally good One. This is not abstract goodness; it is goodness revealed in time and

> only in Christ do we apprehend that order in which we stand and that knowledge of it with which we have been endowed.

Oliver O'Donovan, *Resurrection and Moral Order: An Outline for Evangelical Ethics*, 2nd ed. (Apollos, 1994), 19–20.

17. Bonhoeffer, *Ethics*, 49.

relationally. Jesus demonstrates the good order he has known from eternity in his relation to his Father (John 17:21–24). He also demonstrates God's love for the world he has made, love that extends to eternity past and has its place in the being of God himself (1 John 4:7–21). Jesus, the incarnate Son, makes ultimate goodness concrete.[18]

The Orderer of the world. Second, Jesus is the eternal Son who ordered the world and to whom the world is ordered. Truly, it is "by him all things were created, in heaven and on earth, visible and invisible, whether thrones or dominions or rulers or authorities—all things were created through him and for him" (Col. 1:16). In Jesus Christ, truth itself is made known, not just truth about something, but the truth about all things. Jesus is the reference point for all things, the One in relation to whom all things are relative. Karl Barth wisely identifies this Christocentric reference point for reality: "The truth of Jesus Christ is not one truth among others; it is *the* truth, the universal truth that creates all truth as surely as it is the truth of God, the *prima veritas* which is also the *ultima veritas*."[19]

Like nothing else in the world, Jesus Christ reveals ultimate truth. In Jesus, the eternal enters the temporal; he is the incarnation of divine wisdom. The One who made the world was in the world (John 1:10). Therefore, if we are to know the proper order of things, we look to the One by whom and unto whom all things are ordered.

The Sustainer of the world. Third, Jesus is the eternal Son who sustains the world. Colossians 1:17 tells us that "he is before all things, and in him all things hold together." This notion of "holding together"[20] connotes sustenance through *all* things finding coherence,

18. This is not to say that God's goodness was always known in the abstract before the advent of Christ. I would argue that God's goodness has always been known in the covenants, but Christ comes as the new and ultimate covenant, a perfect demonstration of God's goodness in the created order.

19. Karl Barth, *Dogmatics in Outline* (Harper & Row, 1959), 26.

20. Greek: *synestēken*, third person singular perfect active indicative form of the verb *synistēmi*. The verb signifies ongoing involvement.

endurance, and even existence in him.[21] In other words, all things are and continue to be because of the Son's active agency. Regarding morality, the Son is the one who continues to provide for the cosmos as the sovereign Lord. As such, there is no question to whom the world owes allegiance, as there is no one else on whom the world depends for life. So, while there may be quarrels and competitions, or structures and politics within creation seeking order or power, all creatures can only relate to one another as creatures. And though we may "depend" upon others in a community penultimately, there is only one ultimate Provider, one Creator and Sustainer.

This, of course, is not widely recognized but actively denied by most people in the world (cf. Ps. 2). But popular opinion must not dictate standards of truth. Bonhoeffer considered this concerning the perceived tension and battle for spiritual power. He argues, "The world is not divided between Christ and the devil; it is completely the world of Christ, whether it recognizes this or not. As this reality in Christ it is to be addressed, and thus the false reality that it imagines itself to have, in itself or in the devil, is to be destroyed."[22] Jesus is the beneficent Provider for all that is. Nothing comes to be or remains in existence without his agency.

In this section, we have seen that Jesus is *the* truth as the preeminent Son. I have aimed to demonstrate that Jesus is the ontological foundation for all reality (Job 12:10; Acts 17:24–31; Heb. 2:11). Nothing exists without reference to him, being both created and sustained by him. This ontology was demonstrated to us in the revelation of the eternal Son incarnate in the man Jesus Christ. But what is more, *this* man also showed us that all things are appropriately ordered unto him teleologically, being made through him and for him. Since the world lives in denial of this reality—having "exchanged the truth

21. BDAG entry for *synistēmi*, B3.
22. Bonhoeffer, *Ethics*, 65.

about God for a lie" (Rom. 1:25)—and suffers the curse brought upon it, Jesus came not just in demonstration of teleological order but in fulfillment of it. Jesus Christ is the last Adam.

The Life: The Last Adam

When considering humanity's plight as a result of the fall, we must recognize where humanity has fallen from. Sin, in its first instance, was a failure of humanity to follow the order God had purposed for the world, and in that order for man to fulfill his role in the economy (i.e., the creation). I will not take time here to develop a theological anthropology; that will be my task in chapter 5. I will, however, provide enough of a picture to demonstrate how Christ fulfills humanity's *telos*, an end in which we can participate now and for which we wait in anticipation of the eschatological future.

Fulfillment of humanity's telos: Sabbath/shalom. In the creation of the world, God planned for humanity to participate in his economy as agents bringing completion to the work he began. So, we can say that humanity was made good but not perfect.[23] As we shall see later, protological humanity was made to reach an eschatological identity.[24] Just as the days were ordered with a Sabbath conclusion, humanity was meant to enter into God's rest (Gen. 2:1–3; Heb. 3:11–4:13). The first Adam was given a theologically ordered task to fulfill in the earth until creation reached its consummation. This task was specified as the means to achieving the end; humankind was charged to

23. "Good" is used here with moral overtones, including a particular order. "Perfection" is used without moral reference but instead to signify completion/fullness.

24. Geerhardus Vos, *The Eschatology of the Old Testament*, ed. James T. Dennison Jr. (P&R, 2001), 73–76. See also William Dumbrell, *The Search for Order: Biblical Eschatology in Focus* (Baker, 1994), 21–22. We will engage these concepts of "protological" and "eschatological" man in our chapter on anthropology. For now, it is worth noting that I have borrowed this language from David VanDrunen, *Divine Covenants and Moral Order: A Biblical Theology of Natural Law* (Eerdmans, 2014), 41–42.

"be fruitful and multiply and fill the earth and subdue it, and have dominion over the fish of the sea and over the birds of the heavens and over every living thing that moves on the earth" (Gen. 1:28). In Reformed theology, this responsibility given to humankind by God is identified as the covenant of works.[25] Upon successful fulfillment of this covenant, humankind would reach the consummation of God's purposes for creation: *shalom* and *Sabbath*.

Though humanity failed to achieve the proper ends God had established for his world, God made provision for their ongoing existence. Ultimately God planned for his Son to come as the *last* Adam, humanity's representative head, in order to achieve the telos humanity was destined for. In Christ, humanity reaches eschatological fulfillment—taking us not back to the garden to reinstitute a covenant of works once more but to provide a new creation for us. The new life that we know in Christ, by the Spirit, is a foretaste of this eschatological reality when he will make all things new (Rev. 21:5). "So then, there remains a Sabbath rest for the people of God" (Heb. 4:9).

The ascension and union with Christ. It is significant, but often overlooked, that the risen Christ has ascended to the right hand of the Father, where he reigns until the time of his return to consummate his kingdom. The ascension of Christ is crucial to a host of important moral topics. Most significantly, Christ has sent his Spirit to be his presence with believers and to perfect them in his work. As Michael Horton explains, "Jesus will be with his people in a more intimate way after his ascension than before because his Spirit will live within them and unite them to Christ."[26] Standing as the true vicar of Christ, the Spirit makes Christ present to believers, but also believers present to Christ.[27] Ethically, then, we are to "keep in step with the Spirit"

25. Westminster Confession of Faith, chap. 7.
26. Horton, *Rediscovering the Holy Spirit*, 131.
27. Horton, *Rediscovering the Holy Spirit*, 133.

(Gal. 5:25). The Spirit leads us in new life, transforming us into the likeness of Christ, true and glorious reality (2 Cor. 3:18). Horton points out, "The *more we receive* from the Spirit of the realities of the age to come, the *more restless we become*, having already received a foretaste of the future."[28]

A sure future—promised in the resurrection, fulfilled at the parousia. The great promise of the resurrection is that humanity has a future. This future is marked by affirmation of the goodness of God's creation and indeed the redemption of that created order. But it is also characterized by otherness, being glorious and perfect. Beautifully, then, the biblical vision for the restoration of all things is a vision "to unite all things in Christ, things in heaven and things on earth" (Eph. 1:10). Oliver O'Donovan is correct: "Jesus is not only a witness to the restored moral order, however indispensable; he is the one in whom that order has come to be. God has willed that the restored creation should take form in, and in relation to, one man. He exists not merely as an example of it, not even as a prototype of it, but as the one in whom it is summed up. To participate in the new creation is, not provisionally only but forever, to participate in Christ."[29] This participation in Christ is experienced now in the resurrected life believers know in part, the new life they have as they've been baptized into Christ's death and live in the Spirit (Rom. 6:1–11). Therefore, O'Donovan says, "From the resurrection we look not only back to the created order which is vindicated, but forwards to our eschatological participation in that order. Of that final enjoyment we have a present anticipation through the Pentecostal gift of the Holy Spirit."[30]

In anticipation of this eschatological future, there is a temptation to overreach regarding human responsibility. With humanity's failure, in the eternal wisdom of God, it was ordained that the Son

28. Horton, *Rediscovering the Holy Spirit*, 222.
29. O'Donovan, *Resurrection and Moral Order*, 150.
30. O'Donovan, *Resurrection and Moral Order*, 22.

should take on flesh to bring the cosmos to its proper eschatological end. The work of redemption ordained by the Father, executed in the Son, is being completed in Christ by the Spirit, all to the praise of God's glorious grace (Eph. 1:3–14).[31] But it must be clear that humans (even the elect) are not bringing shalom, nor are they ushering in the kingdom through their cultural activities. David VanDrunen says, "To take such a view is to compromise the finality and sufficiency of Christ's perfect obedience on earth and his glorious entry into the glory of heaven. The new creation has been earned and attained by the work of Christ the last Adam alone."[32] Though the work of humanity isn't bringing eschatological fulfillment, humanity's responsibilities to God, neighbor, and creation are not dismissed. I will return to humanity's cultural responsibilities later in this book.

Conclusion

In this chapter, we've seen that Jesus Christ provides both the ontological and teleological order of morality. All things, properly considered, have a theological reference. The perfect revelation of God and his plans and purposes for humanity are known in the incarnate Christ—the Word made flesh. Much more could be said about how Jesus validates the authority of the Scriptures. But here, I want to emphasize that Jesus is indispensable to our understanding of God,

31. Notice the trinitarian nature of Eph. 1:3–14, as the text is broken up into three sections signaled by repetition of the doxology in vv. 6, 12, 14. Each section focuses on the work of a different Person of the Godhead, working in unison.

32. David VanDrunen, *Living in God's Two Kingdoms: A Biblical Vision for Christianity and Culture* (Crossway, 2010), 164. Christoph Schwöbel applies similar thinking to ecology. Schwöbel, "God, Creation, and the Christian Community: The Dogmatic Basis of a Creation Ethic of Createdness," in *The Doctrine of Creation: Essays in Dogmatics, History and Philosophy*, ed. Colin E. Gunton (T&T Clark, 1997), 150. Cited in Colin Gunton, *The Triune Creator: A Historical and Systematic Study* (Eerdmans, 1998), 228–29.

creation, self, and morality. As O'Donovan says, "True knowledge of the moral order is knowledge 'in Christ.'"[33]

If we are to ever properly understand morality, it will be as we know Jesus. Jesus is the first and the last, for it is by him and for him that all things exist (Col. 1:16). In this chapter, we considered our need for God's intervention in the economy to both reveal and restore moral order. In the next chapter, we consider divine agency and goodness within the Godhead.

33. O'Donovan, *Resurrection and Moral Order*, 85.

2

God and Goodness

> The highest good, than which there is no higher, is God, and consequently He is unchangeable good, hence truly eternal and truly immortal. All other good things are only from Him, not of Him. For what is of Him, is Himself. And consequently if He alone is unchangeable, all things that He has made, because He has made them out of nothing, are changeable.[1]
>
> Saint Augustine

> And Jesus said to him, "Why do you call me good? No one is good except God alone."
>
> Luke 18:19

THERE IS NO MORE IMPORTANT moral question than the relationship of God and goodness. A common childhood prayer serves as a simple dictum on the matter: "God is great, God

An earlier version of this chapter was published as "God and Goodness," *The Global Anglican* 139, no. 3 (October 2025): 257–67.

1. Augustine, *Concerning the Nature of Good, Against the Manicheans* 1 (*NPNF*[1] 4:451).

is good . . ." There is much to respect about the faith associated with such a prayer. The prayer is a declaration of belief in the very character of the God to whom the child prays. But such childlike simplicity of faith can be quickly accused of childlike naïveté. Experience betrays a lack of confidence in the goodness of God when the world is so rife with trouble. Or perhaps there is a lack of confidence in the goodness of God's command when what we want is strictly prohibited under divine law.

The dismissal of the metaphysical is widely recognized, especially following Alasdair MacIntyre, as the seat of modern moral confusion.[2] Theology proper fills this metaphysical void, but the nature of the relationship between God and goodness remains a puzzle within theological ethics. Namely, how does a reckoning of God's goodness, proper to his (uncreated) essence, impact our understanding of creaturely realities? This chapter proposes a retrieval of God's being as the foundation of moral reality. I will begin by considering God's essence *in se* before turning to the divine works *ad extra*. The fundamental difference between uncreated and created beings is shown not to discount moral reality but to serve as its foundation. I will conclude that God's essence guarantees the goodness of the creation and serves as the ultimate reference point for morality.

The Historical "Dilemma"

The question of the relationship between God and goodness is not novel, nor is it exclusively Christian. This is perhaps the most fundamental question philosophers have grappled with for millennia. What is our reference for ultimate good? Is this reference God (or the divine) or something external to God? If it is internal to God (or

2. See Alasdair MacIntyre, *After Virtue: A Study in Moral Theory*, 3rd ed. (University of Notre Dame Press, 2007).

the divine), how do we account for the negative experiences we see in life, or the commands we are uncertain about? Is good whimsical, at the mercy of divine volition? Or, if goodness is external to God (or the divine), does this actually make God less God, as there is something more ultimate?

In *Euthyphro*, Plato explores concerns related to the divine and goodness.[3] In the conversation between Socrates and Euthyphro, as it unfolds in Plato's work, they wrestle the tension of the human experience under the will of the gods. How should we (humans) reckon anything, but especially moral judgments, in view of the divine? They struggle to locate the source of goodness in the pantheon of their religion, seeing tensions in what seemed to be the arbitrary nature of the will of the gods.[4] The dialogue concludes that what is to be determined good is whatever is ultimately pleasing to the gods (12e), but the location of that good (ontologically) never seems to be fixed; rather, it is found in the divine volitions (14b).

The disagreements Christians have with Plato's work are immediately recognized in the tension presented by a plurality of deities.[5] Multiple deities entail multiple wills, and therefore potential for competing goods. Or, if there is a united sense of good, then there is a notion that transcends the divine and is ultimately higher than the deities. Though the matter of the relation of the divine to the good

3. Plato, *Euthyphro*, vol. 1 of *Plato in Twelve Volumes*, trans. Harold North Fowler (Harvard University Press, 1966).

4. The classic summary of the "Euthyphro dilemma" is the question whether something is good because God (or the gods) will it, or if it is willed because it is good. Timothy Chappell challenges this classic interpretation, claiming it is not actually present in Plato's *Euthyphro*. Chappell says what the dilemma entails is not the wills of the gods but the love(s) of the gods. See Chappell, "Euthyphro's 'Dilemma,' Socrates' *Daimonion* and Plato's God," in *God, Goodness and Philosophy*, ed. Harriet A. Harris (Ashgate, 2011), 63–85. Despite this important challenge, I am addressing the classic presentation of the dilemma as it bears upon theistic accounts of goodness.

5. There are also many similarities between the Platonist and Christian (or theist) positions. For more, consider Robert Merrihew Adams, *Finite and Infinite Goods: A Framework for Ethics* (Oxford University Press, 1999), 13–49.

in Plato is different in the pantheon than the monotheism of Christianity, the questions remain: Where is good to be found, particularly with relation to the divine volition? How is good related to God?

In this chapter I will answer these questions theologically, beginning with God's existence *in se*, before considering the relationship of his being to creatures.

God from Eternity

Theological exploration is always recursive. We reflect from our experience and knowledge, but we seek truth about God that is true of God in himself. Our knowledge of God is always contingent on his revelation of himself, but we do not want to limit God to the economy, nor confuse him with it.

Dogmatic exploration of goodness in relationship to God is an exploration of the divine essence, that holy mystery known only in what has been revealed to us. The invitation of the psalmist is to "taste and see that the LORD is good!" (Ps. 34:8).[6] Goodness is the

6. Jaco Gericke claims identifying this psalm in the way I have could be problematic because of the "non-tautological predication of goodness as an extrinsic property of Yhwh based on an alleged synthetic *a posteriori* religious reasoning. . . . [If this is true, then] moral goodness was indeed assumed to be something independent from the deity and with reference to which Yhwh could be called 'good' (or not)." Gericke, "Beyond Divine Command Theory: Moral Realism in the Hebrew Bible," in *God, Goodness and Philosophy*, ed. Harriet A. Harris (Ashgate, 2011), 91. My argument is against Gericke here, based on ontological claims about the divine. I am seeking to identify the *quiddity* of God, which I believe is known in the encounter of God. To say anything known about God is always external to God would be nonsensical and would defeat a concept of the divine altogether, at least in making God's essence in some sense accidental. When we encounter God, we recognize goodness, a concept we've known in some sense *a priori* to this encounter. But the encounter of God as the One who *is* good must be part of the recursive process of all theological reflection. In fact, by encountering God as good, we recognize all we've known to be good has only come to us from him. We do not define God by concepts known external to God but seek to refine our concepts according to the revelation of the God who is before all others. Therefore, my contention is not with his exegesis, per se, but with his lack of theological clarity in interpretation. For a great defense against this sort of predication, see Anselm of Canterbury, *Monologion*, in *The*

quiddity—or the "isness"—of God, essential to his being. So, goodness is an essential attribute of God from eternity, not accidental to him. His goodness is not contingent on the creation, though all goodness in creation is contingent on him. Furthermore, though his goodness is from eternity, he delights in making his goodness known in the creation.

Along with confessing God's singular divine essence (*ousia*), Christian orthodoxy also confesses three divine persons (*hypostases*). The Athanasian Creed captures these truths succinctly: "We worship one God in Trinity, and Trinity in Unity, neither confounding the persons, nor dividing the substance." Modern trinitarian controversies have revisited some historical tensions in the doctrine of the Trinity, emphasizing the relationships of persons as the locus of divine unity, rather than the singular divine essence (i.e., divine simplicity). Such moves have reimagined each of the divine persons with discrete wills. However, the classical position has located the will of God in the singular essence, not the divine persons. Therefore, God as three persons always acts in unity and does so from his essence. God's will accords with and is essential to his being.

That God's goodness and God's will are both located in the essence of God is significant for considering God's relationship to the creation, and our knowledge and experience of goodness. God is good, and God's will is always agreeable to and expressive of ultimate goodness because his goodness and his will are both essential to who he is. So, when God acts, he does so from and in accordance with his own essence (James 1:17). Aquinas captures this relationship of essence and existence: "Since in God there is no potentiality . . . it follows that in Him essence does not differ from existence. Therefore His essence is His existence."[7] Identifying God's perfection (completeness

Major Works: Including Monologion, Proslogion, and Why God Became Man, Oxford World Classics (Oxford University Press, 1998), 1–30.

7. Thomas Aquinas, *Summa Theologica* I, q. 3, a. 4.

or fullness) of existence means that there is no potential in God. If God is good, he is so completely and maximally. Furthermore, if his will is perfect, it is unfailing and unwavering. Therefore, God's goodness is expressed perfectly in his divine will. His being is good, as is his will. They are essential to him, and therefore they are his existence.

These dogmatic convictions have moral implications. Returning to the Euthyphro dilemma, Christians recognize two important truths at the core of reality.[8] First, good is not external to God, a benchmark against which he can be measured. God's essence is good. Second, God's will is not in competition with good, because God's will is essential to him. So, God's will is also good. The conclusion of these two implications is that who God is and what God purposes (and by implication, does—our next consideration) are good. This conclusion is important for any theological reflection on ethics. In fact, when considering the nature of the good and moral obligation for human beings, we must recognize that God is the ontological basis for good before there were any created beings.

We turn now to see how God's good nature gives us confidence to know the goodness of his transitive works in creating and engaging with his creation.

God and the Economy

Having seen that God's goodness and will are essential to his being, we now consider how that being exerts itself beyond itself. Being perfect, God acts of no necessity. Therefore, when God creates, he does so from the fullness of his own being, not making up for any lack in himself. Anything that exists beyond God depends upon God. God is

8. I am seeking here to show how a *dogmatic* account of divine simplicity provides a solution to the Euthyphro dilemma. For a *philosophical* argument to the same end, see Anders Kraal, "Does Divine Simplicity Solve the Euthyphro Dilemma?," in *God, Goodness and Philosophy*, ed. Harriet A. Harris (Ashgate, 2011).

the only one who exists of himself, without cause. God's work outside himself takes effect on things that otherwise would not exist without his willing them to be. The significance for our moral consideration is that all existence comes from God himself.

The confession that God created the universe from nothing is significant at this point. There is only one originating and supreme nature from which all other natures exist.[9] When God acts, he does not engage something to act on, for that would be a preexistent nature that would rival his supreme nature. Instead, as Anselm notes, "everything (except the supreme essence) is made out of nothing, i.e., not out of some thing."[10] Causation, then, is owing to God's initiative and to the work carried forward according to his being. Here again we see God's will and goodness are inextricably linked. "The core of Christian teaching about creation out of nothing is not cosmology or philosophy of nature or anthropology, but the Holy Trinity's perfection and benevolence."[11]

All creatures, as they receive their existence from God, likewise receive goodness from God.[12] All goodness is owing entirely to God. Furthermore, all creatures *know* and *seek* goodness in him. The apostle Paul's address to the Areopagus in the book of Acts made this clear: God made everything in the world (17:24) and he does not depend on anything (17:25). But in his self-sufficiency, God has purposed that all people "should seek God, and perhaps feel their way toward him and find him. Yet he is actually not far from

9. Anselm, *Monologion*, 16.

10. Anselm, *Monologion*, 22.

11. John Webster, "'Love Is also a Lover of Life': *Creatio Ex Nihilo* and Creaturely Goodness," in vol. 1 of *God Without Measure: Working Papers in Christian Theology* (T&T Clark, 2015), 102.

12. Petrus van Mastricht, *Faith in the Triune God*, vol. 2 of *Theoretical-Practical Theology*, ed. Joel R. Beeke, trans. Todd M. Rester (Reformation Heritage, 2019), 332. Mastricht argues along similar lines to Aquinas in *Summa Theologica* I, q. 6. Bavinck would later take up the same line of argument; see Herman Bavinck, *Reformed Dogmatics*, vol. 2, *God and Creation*, ed. John Bolt, trans. John Vriend (Baker Academic, 2004), 212.

each one of us, for 'In him we live and move and have our being'" (17:27–28).

Creation is good because it is the effect of the supreme good, God. But creation is always contingently good, having what it does by derivation from God. Aquinas unpacks this idea: "Everything is therefore called good from the divine goodness, as from the first exemplary effective and final principle of all goodness. Nevertheless, everything is called good by reason of the similitude of the divine goodness belonging to it, which is formally its own goodness, whereby it is denominated good. And so of all things there is one goodness, and yet many goodnesses."[13] We know and experience good in the economy only because there is a reference of that good to the ultimate good. Goodness can be known apart from knowledge of God, to some degree at least, because the creation itself *is* good; its being is good because God made it. There is a recognition of goodness in created effects, even if there is no recognition of the cause of those effects. David captures this well in Psalm 145, praising God for both his common and particular provision. Indeed, "the LORD is good [*tov*] to all" (v. 9). All creation looks to God for provision (vv. 15–16), even if not all creation loves him and many will be destroyed in judgment (v. 20).

But though the creation is good, it is not good in the same sense as God. Creation's goodness can be diminished through denial. Augustine says that for a being to exist, it requires good. Without goodness, a being would cease to exist: "For however small or of whatever kind the being may be, the good which makes it a being cannot be destroyed without destroying the being itself. . . . Corruption can consume the good only by consuming the being."[14] Augustine argues that goodness constituted true being. Evil is a predator upon the good,

13. Aquinas, *Summa Theologica* I, q. 6, a. 4.
14. Augustine, *Enchiridion* 12 (*NPNF*[1] 3:340).

depending upon the good for "existence."[15] Without good, there is no genuine being to corrupt and, therefore, no prospect for evil.[16] Evil is the corruption of the good, a privation of the good.[17]

The questions that naturally arise from our current study are how to account for freedom and actuality regarding God's will. In other words, does the presence of evil—the corruption of the good—overrule God's goodness, particularly his good will for the creation? We turn to consider the providence of God, factoring human rebellion.

The Providence of God

We have seen that creation is good because of God's agency in making and upholding it. Furthermore, to exist necessitates goodness. So how, in the face of this pervasive goodness, do we account for evil in the world? This question is too vast to answer here, but I will at least make some preliminary observations that will better account for the goodness of God as the foundation of moral reality.

The classical position regarding the good, both philosophically and theologically, was to identify the highest good with what is most desirable. Aristotle begins his *Nicomachean Ethics* by acknowledging that all endeavors (e.g., inquiry, action, choice) aim at some good.[18] So, good is the end each endeavor seeks. He concludes, "If, then, there is some end of the things we do, which we desire for its own sake (everything else being desired for the sake of this), and if we do not

15. Aquinas agrees with Augustine in terms of being as fundamentally good: "No being can be spoken of as evil, formally as being, but only so far as it lacks being. Thus a man is said to be evil, because he lacks some virtue; and an eye is said to be evil, because it lacks the power to see well." Aquinas, *Summa Theologica* I, q. 5, a. 3.

16. Augustine, *Enchiridion* 14 (*NPNF*[1] 3:341).

17. Augustine, *On the Nature of Good,* chaps. 16–17.

18. Aristotle, *Nicomachean Ethics*, ed. Lesley Brown, trans. David Ross, Oxford World's Classics (Oxford University Press, 2009), 1.1.

choose everything for the sake of something else (for at that rate the process would go on to infinity, so that our desire would be empty and vain), clearly this must be the good and the chief good."[19] Desire was crucial to the identification of the good.

Similarly, Augustine recognizes the significance of desire to our reckoning of the good. In his *Enchiridion*, he denies that God was the author of evil. Why was Adam and Eve's eating of the forbidden fruit sinful? It was not because God had planted an evil tree. Instead, it was because Adam chose a lesser good than God. "Man did not therefore strive after an evil nature when he touched the forbidden tree; but by deserting what was better, he committed an evil deed. . . . God did not plant an evil tree in Paradise; but He Himself was better who prohibited its being touched."[20] Augustine shows the wrongness of *desiring* something above God. True good, that which is highest, is that which is most desirable. By failing to desire properly, Adam sinned. His desire was a corruption of the good. His sin was not that he loved the creature but that he worshiped (i.e., loved and esteemed more highly) the creature rather than the Creator (Rom. 1:21–25).

Later medieval scholars and many Reformed theologians after them would develop similar positions regarding desire and goodness. Thomas Aquinas tells us that God, as the first cause, is the preeminent goodness and most desirable.[21] John Duns Scotus contends that God always loves the divine essence and always has the divine essence as the primary object of his will. So, when God wills to create (of no necessity), he orders that creation in accordance with his own divine goodness, the primary good.[22] Similarly, and much later, Herman Bavinck argues: "Inasmuch as he himself is the absolutely good

19. Aristotle, *Nicomachean Ethics*, 1.2.

20. Augustine, *Enchiridion* 34 (*NPNF*[1] 3:358).

21. Aquinas, *Summa Theologica* I, q. 6, a. 1.

22. See the discussion of Duns Scotus in John E. Hare, *God's Call: Moral Realism, God's Commands, and Human Autonomy* (Eerdmans, 2001), 76. Hare engages a breadth of Duns Scotus's material, including *Ordinatio* I d.10, *Ordinatio* III d.8, and *Reportatio Parisiensis I-A*.

and perfect one, he may not love anything else except with a view to himself. He may not and cannot be content with less than absolute perfection. When he loves others, he loves himself in them: his own virtues, works, and gifts. For the same reason he is also blessed in himself as the sum of all goodness, of all perfection."[23] The principal good always provides a teleological orientation to creation. God himself desires what is highest, and orders our good to this end.

We now begin to see the payload of what we have been considering. We would be tempted to cry foul at God because of the experience of evil under the Lord's sovereign rule. However, evil is not a being but the corruption of being by agents (humans and angels) with some freedom. But this freedom to choose against the good is not a compromise of the good. The grand mystery is that God, in his sovereign providence, allows and uses evil for good. Augustine captures this paradox marvelously:

> God does well even in the permission of what is evil. For He permits it only in the justice of His judgment. And surely all that is just is good. Although, therefore, evil, in so far as it is evil, is not a good; yet the fact that evil as well as good exists, is a good. For if it were not a good that evil should exist, its existence would not be permitted by the omnipotent Good, who without doubt can easily refuse to permit what He does not wish, as bring about what He does wish.[24]

Augustine's claim seems audacious at first glance, saying it is good that God permits evil. However, this is not a naïve or irreverent statement. Instead, it is theologically principled and marked by immense faith. Augustine begins with theological truth before moving to experience. If God is good, and all that God wills is good, then whatever is evil must have some good purpose in God's grand and

23. Bavinck, *Reformed Dogmatics*, 2:211.
24. Augustine, *Enchiridion* 96 (*NPNF*[1] 3:367).

mysterious plan for his creation. The guarantee of this good is the good God himself, who wills and works all things according to his good purposes.

Conclusion

If God is the source of all goodness and the reference for what is truly good, then we have some metaphysical foundation for morality. There is an original and preeminent good that is absolute. This good serves as the guarantee of moral order. All things are ordered unto the ultimate good. Even when evil corrupts the good, God, in his sovereignty, uses evil for good. This is *not* a declaration of evil as good but a recognition that evil intentions cannot stop or compromise God's good plans. In fact, this evil only happens by divine permission.

In this chapter, I have not explored formal theories of theological voluntarism or divine command theory (or any other formal theory, for that matter). But what I have explored, especially dogmatically, has a bearing upon any metaethics. If morality requires a reference, and ethics is fundamentally a question of the good—even as it bears on what may be right or wrong—then there is no higher standard than God, who is the ultimate good. As we engage in the economy, we recognize that all being is good and ordered to the good. Evil is a corruption of the good, a denial of what is. But God, being sovereign, uses even evil for his good purposes.

So, a theological account of reality offers great consolation to those of faith. Puritan preacher Thomas Watson gives this encouragement: "Learn to adore Providence. Providence has an influence upon all things here below. It is this that mingles the ingredients, and makes up the whole compound."[25] If God wills only good, then

25. Thomas Watson, *All Things for Good* (Banner of Truth, 1986), 3.2.1.

even the most difficult of circumstances will work for good. The confession of those living by faith is found in the Epistle to the Romans: "And we know that for those who love God all things work together for good, for those who are called according to his purpose" (Rom. 8:28).

3

A Good Place

What the Creator Created

It is a great and very rare thing for a man, after he has contemplated the whole creation, corporeal and incorporeal, and has discerned its mutability, to pass beyond it, and, by the continued soaring of his mind, to attain to the unchangeable substance of God, and, in that height of contemplation, to learn from God Himself that none but He has made all that is not of the divine essence.[1]

Saint Augustine

Christian dogmatics . . . precisely because it talks of God, and of all other matters in the light of God, will not rest content with descriptions of contingent moral culture.[2]

John Webster

1. Augustine, *The City of God* 11.2 (*NPNF*[1] 2:206–6).

2. John Webster, "God and Conscience," in *Word and Church: Essays in Christian Dogmatics* (T&T Clark, 2001), 245.

We are often required to distinguish between good things to make a decision. For instance, if you have limited resources, what is more important, a new watch or paying the power bill? This example may seem trivial, but these decisions begin to matter more and more when life is at stake. Most would agree that life matters more than material goods that furnish life, though most would also say that quality of life is significant. But *what* is living also matters. If you have to decide between feeding your dog or feeding your child, which do you choose? Intuitively, most people would care for a child before a pet. But they may not be able to answer *why* this is so. As we make decisions in life, we need a basis for knowing what kinds of things we are engaging with and what they are for. Only then will our decisions be responsible and moral.

In the last chapter, we explored the fount of all goodness, God. Here, we turn to consider all things external to God. Dogmatically, creation belongs to the *opera ad extra*, the action of God outside his inner life. All that is not God is created, for God is the only uncreated. Although the creation is not God, it is still good because God willed and acted to bring it to being. In this chapter, we will explore creation as the free act of the triune God in love. We will identify an inherent moral order identifiable in the generic and telic ordering God has established. This order will serve as the basis for moral judgments and deliberation later.

In the Beginning, God

John Webster explores two dimensions of God's goodness in relation to the creation of the cosmos. First, creation was not a physical act, but rather an ethical one. The creation does not emerge from some physicality of God, but from his goodness—in the metaphysical sense, his fully realized nature, or perfection. This means that creation is not a means to an end, filling up some lack in the divine life. God's triune being enjoys eternal beatitude. It is in this fullness that God can create freely and provide creation with a free existence. There is a call to the creation to delight in the Creator, who eternally delights in his own divine life. The creation is to accord with this proper and ultimate end, but if it fails to do so, it is of no detriment to the Creator. God's delight in the creation is seeing it enjoy what he knows and enjoys fully from eternity—his divine goodness.[3]

Second, the morality of God's act of creation is seen from this fullness in that there is no competition for God. His goodness is not threatened in creation, as if it can be expended or rivaled. Rather, from the perfection of his goodness, he is free to make other beings that are, after his likeness, completely good. He does not lose or gain in creating. He creates for the benefit of others, sharing the goodness that is completely his. So, in creating a good moral order, there is no consequence to himself—thus, he is impassible.[4]

That God does not need to create has led to much speculation about why he would create. Rather than expounding the various positions and arguments here, I will limit consideration to a widely held Reformed position—a biblical and Augustinian position before the Reformed—on the end for which the world was made.

The shorter and larger Westminster Catechisms begin with the question of the chief end of humanity. While this question is not directly posited with relation to the entire cosmos, the fundamental concern is with the responsibility of humanity, the pinnacle of

3. Webster captures the moral dimension of the creation in his reflection on what is implied by God creating from his will, without compulsion. This, while being free, is an act according to nature and therefore the divine ethos. Creation accords with God's supreme generosity on the basis of his eternal love of himself in the divine processions. John Webster, "Trinity and Creation," in vol. 1 of *God Without Measure: Working Papers in Christian Theology* (T&T Clark, 2015), 93.

4. See John Webster, "'Love Is Also a Lover of Life': *Creatio Ex Nihilo* and Creaturely Goodness," in vol. 1 of *God Without Measure: Working Papers in Christian Theology* (T&T Clark, 2015), 104; and Webster, "Trinity and Creation," 92.

the cosmos (cf. Gen. 1:26–31; Ps. 8; Heb. 2:5–18). The catechisms' answer is, "To glorify God and enjoy him forever." This dictum is widely known and recited, but it remains unclear whether it is properly understood in practice. Glorifying God does not in any way *add* to God anything he is lacking. Instead, it is an invitation to revel in the fullness of God's goodness. Practically speaking, this means the alignment of creaturely life to divine purposes. "Enjoyment," in the catechisms, is as much a clarifying remark as it is a complementary one. Creatures glorify God *by* enjoying him.

In the eighteenth century, Jonathan Edwards offered arguably the most sophisticated theological treatise on the matter in his *Dissertation Concerning the End for Which God Created the World.* Edwards compares the creation to light emanating from and reflecting back to a source.[5] By employing this analogy, Edwards aims to capture the single divine end in God's works. In sharing his glory externally (*ad extra*), God is only giving what he already possesses internally, and "though God, in seeking this end, seeks the creature's good; yet therein appears his supreme regard to himself."[6] Edwards believes the analogy of light shining from and returning to its source preserves the fact that even in acting beyond himself, God was still the ultimate source of his fullness. The benefit of the creation is not to the divine, then, but to the creature, even if in ultimate service of the divine. In other words, God's act of creating is the sharing of his goodness beyond himself, something that is possible in the freedom of his perfection.[7]

5. Edwards uses the language of emanation and remanation. Jonathan Edwards, "A Dissertation Concerning the End for Which God Created the World," in vol. 1 of *The Works of Jonathan Edwards*, ed. Edward Hickman (Banner of Truth, 1974), 120. For a caution against some of the dangers of arbitrariness with the language of emanation, though not directly targeted at Edwards, see Webster, "Trinity and Creation," 93.

6. Edwards, "End for Which God Created the World," 1:120.

7. Edwards says God's disposition to emanate his goodness and glory is something proper to God (i.e., the divine will). However, Edwards insists that creation was not

The reason I have paused to consider the purpose and cause of creation is to once more theologically frame the moral order. Creation, and therefore the moral order of that creation, has an end (telos). The end of creation is God's glory. God does not receive anything from his creation, but rather, in his benevolence he shares his goodness with others. Because creation issues from the fullness of God's being, creation's highest good is to enjoy the Creator's goodness. This is most clearly expressed in an ordered existence. This ordering takes shape, as we'll now turn to see, in the distinction of both kinds and ends.

Created Order: Generic and Telic

The opening chapters of Genesis provide the theological key, as on a map, to the basic questions of existence. Creation is not only made from nothing (as implied in Gen. 1:1), but it is ordered for the flourishing of life. The creation narrative is told in beautiful poetry, not intended necessarily to be six twenty-four-hour periods (though this is certainly a legitimate reading), but rather to demonstrate a purposeful pattern of forming and filling.[8] On the first three days of creation (Gen. 1:3–13), God forms through separation, thus ordering chaos to prepare places. On the fourth to sixth days (Gen. 1:14–31), the formed places are filled. God provides all that is required for life in his cosmos. He gives both being and purpose to everything. It is this creation of all beings with their purpose that I will now explore as fundamental to the *moral* order.

necessary for God's actualization. God created from his infinite perfection. "Therefore, to speak according to truth, we may suppose, *that a disposition in God, as an original property of his nature, to an emanation of his own infinite fulness, was what excited him to create the world; and so, that the emanation itself was aimed at by him as a last end of the creation.*" Edwards, "End for Which God Created the World," 1:100.

8. Notice the correlation of days: one and four—heaven is formed then populated; two and five—the waters are formed then populated; three and six—the earth is formed (with vegetation) then populated.

Creation fundamentally is ordered according to kinds and ends, or *generic* and *telic* orders (respectively).[9] These orders stand alongside one another within the cosmos, as God is unlike any other kind (*sui generis*) and is the ultimate end of all. Therefore, our consideration of the created *moral* order is specifically for *creatures*.[10] Within creation we can relate creatures generically (by kind) and teleologically (by purpose). An illustration will help to make this clear. A human being is distinct from an animal. Both are distinct from plants. We can categorize each broader category more specifically, such as humans by ethnicity, plants by how they reproduce, animals by whether they are vertebrates or not, and so on. Biologically, this is known as taxonomy. But this distinction by kind is not only significant to science; it also is fundamental to morality. In particular, knowing *what* something is equips us to understand its value and place within an ordered existence and acts as the foundation for systems of justice.[11]

Perhaps more significant morally than separating creatures by kind is the distinction of purpose. Again, vegetables may be said to be *purposed for* food for animals and humans. Telic ordering is less simple to categorize than generic ordering. Kinds can be observed, but purpose less so. To provide an example, one might, for the first time, discover a fork and classify it as a tool or utensil but may struggle to know

9. This sort of classification is not new or distinctively Christian. Ancient philosophy formulated such systems, both in the Platonic and Aristotelian schools. Of the more robust *theological* treatments, which critically engages philosophy, see Thomas Aquinas, *Summa Contra Gentiles, Book Two: Creation*, trans. James F. Anderson (University of Notre Dame Press, 1956), 39–45, 115–39. For another theological treatment, consider Jonathan Edwards, "Miscellaneous Remarks on Important Theological Controversies: Of God's Moral Government," in vol. 2 of *The Works of Jonathan Edwards* (Banner of Truth, 1974), 512.

10. I have considered above how God is engaged "morally" with the creation: He creates from his perfect goodness and remains the standard and source of all goodness.

11. Oliver O'Donovan, *Resurrection and Moral Order: An Outline for Evangelical Ethics*, 2nd ed. (Apollos, 1994), 46.

if its intended use is for combing hair or eating food. *Intention*, in the previous sentence, is key, for it communicates an ordered design with an inherent purpose. When considering tools, we may ask the craftsman. But when thinking more cosmologically, we must hear from the Creator. Hence, a revelation of order becomes necessary.

We should not overlook the significance of how kinds and ends are related. In moral realism—which I believe a biblical faith requires—there must be a correlation of kinds and ends. Without such a correlation, there cannot be a "reality" of moral order, only relativity that is bound to the human will; humans must choose a moral reality rather than make choices in accordance with a given order. This voluntarism is a denial of the Creator, as we will see in the next chapter exploring the nature of sin.[12] However, voluntarism is precisely what has dominated post-Enlightenment moral philosophy. For example, David Hume could not naturally correlate morality with the nature of being, believing morality is bound to the affections and, therefore, the will. Thus, there is no *natural* connection to be discerned between what *is* and what *ought* to be.[13] Once more we see the significance of the metaphysical, and not simply the natural, for a system of morality. In particular, there is a supernatural ordering of the cosmos, "a reference point outside the network of kinds and ends in nature, which nature as a whole is ordered-to-serve and which determines what the flourishing of that natural order is to be."[14] The introductory chapters of Genesis are indispensable for ascertaining the created moral order, for there we see how the world was formed.

12. For a more extensive exploration of moral realism over against voluntarism, see O'Donovan, *Resurrection and Moral Order*, 45–52. Rufus Black gives a thorough treatment of this matter with insightful comments on O'Donovan's position. See Black, *Christian Moral Realism: Natural Law, Narrative, Virtue, and the Gospel* (Oxford University Press, 2000), especially 119–20.

13. See David Hume, *A Treatise on Human Nature*, ed. David Fate Norton and Mary J. Norton (Oxford University Press, 2000), 3.1.1, especially 293–300.

14. O'Donovan, *Resurrection and Moral Order*, 35.

Generically, the Lord created each living creature according to its "kind" (Hebrew *min*; Greek *genos*). This word is repeated during each instance of new life (italicized for emphasis):

> And God said, "Let the earth sprout vegetation, plants yielding seed, and fruit trees bearing fruit in which is their seed, each according to its *kind*, on the earth." And it was so. The earth brought forth vegetation, plants yielding seed according to their own *kinds*, and trees bearing fruit in which is their seed, each according to its *kind*. And God saw that it was good. (Gen. 1:11–12)

> So God created the great sea creatures and every living creature that moves, with which the waters swarm, according to their *kinds*, and every winged bird according to its *kind*. And God saw that it was good. (Gen. 1:21)

> And God said, "Let the earth bring forth living creatures according to their *kinds*—livestock and creeping things and beasts of the earth according to their *kinds*." And it was so. And God made the beasts of the earth according to their *kinds* and the livestock according to their *kinds*, and everything that creeps on the ground according to its *kind*. And God saw that it was good. (Gen. 1:24–25)

The refrain is that each creature was made according to its kind, yet it is not said literally that humanity is made in kind. Instead, it is implied humanity is a kind of its own, male and female in the image of God (Gen. 1:26–27).[15] This like-kind is crucial in Genesis 2 when God creates a partner for the man. The animals are not suited to

15. Matthews notes the significance of this single kind for humanity: "The text's silence . . . infers that mankind is only of one kind. Since humanity is only of one sort, the unity of the human race is prominently noted and, concomitantly, dismisses any notion that certain peoples are inherently superior or inferior." Kenneth A. Matthews, *Genesis 1–11:26*, vol. 1a of the New American Commentary Series (Broadman & Holman, 1996), 174.

the man, being of a different kind (1:20). Thus, God creates woman from man (1:21–22). It is the woman's likeness to man in kind that is celebrated by the man (1:23). Here, humanity is ordered alongside one another, male and female, generically.

Teleologically, Genesis provides a rudimentary hierarchical structure for creaturely existence. This order is easy to miss in the opening chapter, as *ends* are only specifically mentioned with relation to plants (Gen. 1:30–31, italicized for emphasis):

> And God said, "Behold, I have given you every plant yielding seed that is on the face of all the earth, and every tree with seed in its fruit. You shall have them *for* food. And to every beast of the earth and to every bird of the heavens and to everything that creeps on the earth, everything that has the breath of life, I have given every green plant *for* food." And it was so.

However, there is also an implicit ordering of animals unto humans (or in subjection to humans) within God's mandate to humanity. Whereas the animals have the responsibility to "be fruitful and multiply and fill" (1:22) like humanity, humans are charged uniquely as divine image bearers with the task of subduing the earth and having dominion over the other creatures (1:26, 28).

Some have contended that it is precisely the capacity for dominion that constitutes the image of God (*imago Dei*) in humanity. This is the position of Gregory of Nyssa in his treatise *On the Making of Man*.[16] While I agree that the command and the faculties to execute this command are part of image-bearing, I do not believe this is the sum total. I will give further attention to this in chapter 5. For now,

16. Gregory of Nyssa, *On the Making of Man* 6.1 (*NPNF*[2] 5:390–91). Gregory comments especially on the royal rule of humanity. Interestingly, while he specifies the dominion element, he is clear that this dominion is to be carried forward with virtue. So, there is an incorporation of righteousness, not simply rule, in Gregory's theology of humanity and the *imago Dei*.

it is important to see that this charge to have dominion is integral to humanity's unique place within creation. It is an *end* exclusive to human*kind*. In fact, what is crucial to proper dominion by humanity is its recognition of a higher principle or purpose; humanity dominates the earth because, under God, humanity represents God over the earth.

It is worth noting that within humanity, as a single *kind*, there is differentiation among the sexes. This differentiation is not hierarchical in a qualitative sense. Ontologically, in their *being*, man and woman are both created in the image of God. However, there is an ordering *to* that is present among this single kind. Men and women can share ontological status—equality of being—while having different functions. In this way, we might say that woman was made *for* man, and man appropriately *for* woman. The partnership and companionship that would mitigate man's loneliness were not found among the other *kinds* of creatures (Gen. 2:18–20). Indeed, there was no helper fit for him. Only a woman, of the same kind, could fulfill the purpose of helping the man. And yet, she was different from him in a way that was suitable to his need. She complemented him and therefore served as the one who could appropriately be united to him as one flesh (Gen. 2:24), and thus populate and cultivate civilization on the earth.[17]

Having noted the generic and telic ordering of the Genesis account, we can simplify the structure. In its most basic form, we

17. This one-flesh union identifies the proper ordering of sexual relations. This standard of sexual morality is evident in later biblical teaching. For instance, Lev. 18 prohibits incest and homosexuality, both prohibitions that could be argued from Gen. 2:24. Furthermore, Jesus's teaching on divorce in Mark 10:6–9 and Matt. 19:4–9 directly cite Gen. 2:24 as the moral foundation for marriage and divorce (and, therefore, remarriage and adultery). The apostle Paul identifies the sexual union of husband and wife as more than just a creational ordinance, but in fact a sign of an eschatological reality when Christ will be united to his church. This metaphorical identification elevates the moral importance of this paradigmatic union's sanctity.

observe *kinds* that each serve *ends*.[18] God is unlike any other and the end of all. Under God, humanity serves as a unique *kind*, bearing the image of God and tasked with ruling as God's vice-regents or deputies over the creation. Under humanity is the animals. Finally, the vegetation serves as food for plants and animals.

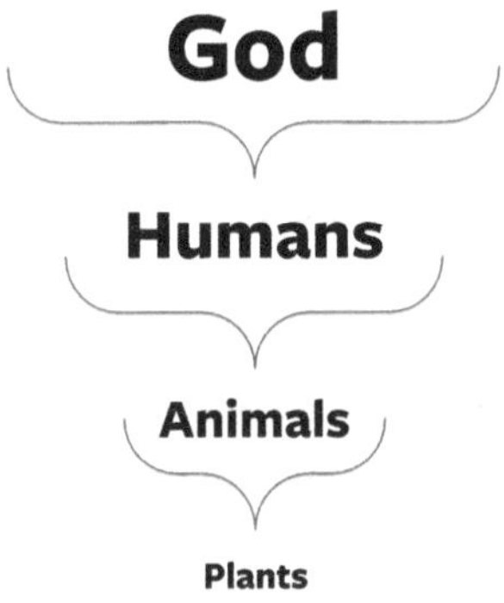

The hierarchical order of life.

We will see the significance of this structured order for morality in the next chapter, as this order is overturned at the fall. For now, we turn to consider how this order served the initial call of humanity to righteous living.

And God Saw That It Was Very Good

The purpose of humanity among the other kinds of creatures is enacted in the dramatic unfolding of the creation story. Structurally, the Genesis narrative is marked out by genealogies, beginning after the introduction (1:1–2:3) with the "generations" (Hebrew *toledot*)

18. Augustine gives an interesting account of the distinction of created reality according to kinds and end. See *City of God* 11.16.

of the cosmos. The conclusion of the previous section—the poetic telling of the seven days of creation—culminates in God blessing the day and making it holy because of God's rest from his work (2:3). Many have remarked on the character of this day of rest, later to be commemorated as the Sabbath day. God, in resting from his work, anticipates the completion of creation at its eschatological end. Creation was made good, but not perfect (i.e., complete). Humanity's place in the creation was to exercise its role as vice-regents to bring the creation to its proper end.[19]

As God made humanity, he charged them to live according to purpose: "Be fruitful and multiply and fill the earth and subdue it, and have dominion over the fish of the sea and over the birds of the heavens and over every living thing that moves on the earth" (Gen. 1:28). The fullness of creation would be realized as humanity populated and cultured the world. The animals would also populate the world with their kind, but humanity alone would rule. The humans as divine image bearers were uniquely tasked with seeing God's creative vision to completion. If they assumed their right place in the created order, they would lead the world to right worship and to the glorious end of Sabbath.

So, as the story continues (or begins), we're told of the first moments of creation when man is given his place and charged with his responsibility. God puts man in the garden of Eden to work and keep it (Gen 2:15). Further, man is invited to name the animals that God created (vv. 19–20), thereby exercising dominion over the animals

19. I will explore more of this teleological dimension of the creation of humanity in chapter 5. For now, I commend several useful resources that explore this facet of creation: Kelly M. Kapic, "Anthropology," in *Christian Dogmatics: Reformed Theology for the Church Catholic*, ed. Michael Allen and Scott R. Swain (Baker Academic, 2016); David VanDrunen, *Living in God's Two Kingdoms* (Crossway, 2010), 33–71; David VanDrunen, *Divine Covenants and Moral Order: A Biblical Theology of Natural Law* (Eerdmans, 2014), 39–94; Michael Horton, *The Christian Faith: A Systematic Theology for Pilgrims on the Way* (Zondervan Academic, 2011), 381–87.

and helping to bring order. In both tasks, man is invited to accept and enact the role of the image-bearer over the creation.

In view of the call to this work, God gives the first command to man: "You may surely eat of every tree of the garden, but of the tree of the knowledge of good and evil you shall not eat, for in the day that you eat of it you shall surely die" (Gen 2:16).[20] This command has been identified as the probationary test for man in the garden. As the man would exercise his right place *over* the plants and the animals, he would need to do so remembering his place *under* God. And so, the command to abstain from eating the fruit was a call to faith and obedience.

What about the "problem" of the serpent's presence (Gen. 3), along with the tree that was not "good" for the man to eat? The best explanation for these is not to doubt the goodness of God's creation but to see them as marks of God's good design. God creates humanity with genuine agency. For this agency to be exercised, there needed to be a single command to obey. If humanity would obey that command, they would express a genuine faith in God and his goodness shown to them.[21] If humanity would disobey, they would demonstrate their lack of faith in God's goodness and their choice to live against reality, as we'll see in the next chapter. Here we observe the command

20. There is a longstanding debate as to whether animals were permitted for eating by humans before the fall. The first mention of animals *for* food was after the flood (Gen. 9:3). Meredith Kline believes that eating animals was permissible from the beginning, citing 1 Tim. 4:3–5 and 2 Pet. 2:12. Irrespective of whether or not animals were permitted/prohibited as food for humans in a prelapsarian context, Kline is right to notice: "Specific mention of plants as food [Gen 1:29] prepares for the special prohibition of the tree of knowledge (2:16, 17)." Kline, *Genesis: A New Commentary*, ed. Jonathan G. Kline (Hendrickson, 2016), 13.

21. "If the inherent nature of good and evil had been drawn into the scope of the test, then it would have resulted in a choice from instinct alone rather than in a choice of a deliberate character. But it was precisely the purpose of the probation to raise man for a moment from the influence of his own ethical inclination to the point of a choosing for the sake of personal attachment to God alone." Geerhardus Vos, *Biblical Theology: Old and New Testaments* (Banner of Truth, 1975), 32.

represented the most basic way that humanity could recognize their proper place as agents under God and over creation. The fruit was not *bad*; trusting God's provision and prohibition was *good*.

The call to trust God as Father and Creator is central to a right recognition of reality and righteousness. The simple command God first gave humanity touches the core of so many moral issues that have arisen throughout history. Consider the idolatrous practices of the pagan nations surrounding Israel. The prophet Isaiah contrasts the false worship of idols with the true worship of YHWH. The irony that runs throughout Isaiah's message is that YHWH is the Creator of all (Isa. 45:12), yet some choose to create gods for themselves (44:9–20). Idolators must carry their gods, even on the backs of animals (46:1–2), and yet YHWH has carried his people even from before their birth (46:3–4). The constant refrain in Isaiah's proclamation is that YHWH alone is God; there is no other. God's people are constantly called to remember this truth: There is *One* who has formed all that is, and his purposes will come to pass (46:8–10). This message is similar to what the apostle Paul would later write in his Epistle to the Romans. God's wrath comes on all unrighteousness, at the core of which is a denial of the truth (Rom. 1:18) leading to false worship (1:22–24). God's place over the world has been known and perceived since creation, leaving humanity without excuse (1:19–20).

We should, therefore, conclude that one simple command given to recognize a fundamental order within the creation serves as a crucial guide to morality. According to Allen Ross, creation "lays the foundation for the law, God's word to his people."[22] Not only is the creation account foundational but what follows is consistent with it. In the coming chapters, we will observe that the *natural law*—as evidenced in the created order and affirmed elsewhere—accords with

22. Allen P. Ross, *Creation and Blessing: A Guide to the Study and Exposition of Genesis* (Baker, 1998), 102.

the *divine law* God gave to his people. The moral order has constancy and integrity because it is theologically determined. I will now briefly examine how the moral order, including creation's goodness, persists even after the fall.

A New Creation

Humanity's rejection of God's moral order brought a curse on the cosmos (Gen. 3:1–19), something we'll consider at greater length in the next chapter. This sin and curse brought the need for the redemption of the world. The question of *what* exactly the creation needed for liberation is significant when thinking about the nature of things, the possibility of righteousness, and the future. For instance, if the creation itself is now materially bad, it would need liberation from the material realm—something akin to Platonism. Or, if the curse doesn't extend in any universal way, then there may be a *natural* possibility of righteousness—something akin to Pelagianism. However, the biblical witness and Christian orthodoxy make it clear that the entirety of the cosmos is completely affected by sin (therefore, not able naturally to choose or live righteously) and that the future is not immaterial but material (therefore, not something to be abandoned or escaped).

We discover the nature of redemption in the provision of the Redeemer. In the death of the incarnate Son and his resurrection to bodily life, we see the culmination of God's plans for his creation. Just as the judgment of the flood was total, yet did not dispense with the creation, so too is the ultimate judgment and new creation. Jesus has judged sin definitively in human flesh, overcoming the curse of sin through his own being cursed by hanging on a tree (Gal. 3:13). The result of Christ's death is the conquest of death itself. Furthermore, the resurrection of Christ in real bodily flesh demonstrates that the new creation is not de novo. Rather, the resurrection of Christ signals to us the nature of the new creation—it is creation transformed. Oliver O'Donovan notes, "The eschatological transformation of the world is neither the mere repetition of the created world nor its negation. It is its fulfilment, its *telos* or end. It is the historical *telos* of the origin, that which creation is intended *for*, and that which it points and strives *towards*."[23] How fitting it is that the One through whom and for whom creation was made (Col. 1:16) should bring creation to its final end: himself.

Conclusion

In this chapter, we have examined the goodness of the creation made by the good Creator. In the freedom of his perfection, God made the world truly good. Inherent to this good world is a divinely designated order, with humanity as the pinnacle of creation purposed for ruling the world in God's image. Though this order was upset by humanity's free choice against the good, the creation remains good nonetheless, even if cursed. Graciously, though humanity has rebelled, God has purposed to redeem humanity and the cosmos. This redemption, provided through the death and resurrection of the incarnate Son, will bring the creation to its ultimate end. Christ is ruling in the heavens now, preparing for the day when he will return to consummate his kingdom, executing justice and making all things new. This "newness" will be a purification of the world, remaking it into what it was purposed to be.

For humans to properly grasp what is best for life in this world, we must first and foremost appreciate *whose* world it is. Order in this world is not arbitrary; it is not something to be determined by individuals. It is an order that God himself ordained. For humanity to rightly assume our place in this world, we must understand whom we

23. O'Donovan, *Resurrection and Moral Order*, 55.

were created for. Allegiance is owed to none other than the Lord, for besides him there is no God. And yet, humanity has chosen against this order in spite of God since the beginning. Having considered the good order of the world, we turn in the next chapter to examine the disorder ensuant from humanity's rebellion.

4

The Nature of Sin

Choosing Our Own Order

> Transgression can only allure in a world of distortion and dreamlike fantasy, where what is real becomes malleable, capable of seeming to be what it is not. . . . We can consistently desire what is bad when we imagine that it will add up to something good, a mental operation only possible if we are deceived about reality.[1]
>
> R. R. Reno

OUR EXPLORATION THUS FAR HAS given us a foundation for determining what is good. We have seen that this goodness is theologically determined. Of course, as moral beings, we know that while a good order may be discerned intellectually, our experience is of great disorder. We know much that is *not* good, indeed evil. To better account for this experience, this chapter explores the nature of sin. I begin with an examination of moral choice and human freedom,

1. R. R. Reno, *Genesis*, BTCB (Brazos, 2010), 85.

examining human agency in the garden of Eden and the ramifications of *that* choice on the rest of the created order. The great challenge to morality has always been *faith*—do we trust that God is good and that his ways are right? Faith is the great difficulty of our subjective experience. Juxtaposing the life of faith with self-determination, I consider the consequences of sin: a creation groaning, a curse, and a disordered cosmos. Ultimately, regeneration alone liberates the sinner from perpetual failure to apprehend true value by restoring true order and orientation to life.

Agency

In considering the nature of sin, we begin with the freedom of the first humans to act. We have been considering the *goodness* of the creation and the order within it. Human beings, in particular, were purposed for dominion over the rest of the creation. To exercise this dominion, they were given a rudimentary frame for their proper place in the created order, marked especially by the single command restricting their eating from the tree of the knowledge of good and evil. As we saw in the previous chapter, this command gave orientation to humanity's freedom, providing a genuine opportunity to express faith by obedience to God. Thus, they would rule and exercise dominion, but always under the rule and dominion of God.

Agency—the ability to act—requires a certain level of freedom, for without free choice, an act results from coercion. In such an instance, it is difficult to discern if it was the actor's responsibility or the one coercing the action. Freedom guarantees the integrity of action—it truly is the act of the agent. This freedom is most important when considering whose fault sin is.[2] I will consider later in this chapter the

2. The conversation about the nature of human freedom is much too vast to cover in detail here. My purpose is to set forward a constructive account in the context of morality. However, there are several treatments of this conversation worth mentioning,

responsibility of human beings after the fall of Adam and Eve. But here, the principal concern is the responsibility of the *first* human agents.[3] These humans, in their original state, were truly free.[4]

Throughout this book, I have identified the problem of moral systems detached from an objective order. The expression of agency, ironically in pursuit of a freely determined moral order, is integral to modern moral chaos. Charles Taylor notes, "Modern freedom was won by our breaking loose from older moral horizons. People used to see themselves as part of a larger order. . . . Modern freedom came about through the discrediting of such orders."[5] Taylor believes instrumental reason has replaced a higher order, seeking to impose an order on how things are and should be. When detached from a given order, this imposition of an order ends up serving individuals. In this way, the moral order becomes broadly voluntaristic. There is no distinction or hierarchy of beings within such a system (or competing systems). Each being's significance and purpose are determined by the will of the moral authority—the individual. Indeed, *individual freedom* is the highest value of this system. But this freedom demands relativism, for no individual will consider themselves truly free when they are told the action they've chosen is wrong. So,

---

particularly with reference to the Reformed tradition. See Richard Muller, *Divine Will and Human Choice* (Baker Academic, 2017); Paul Helm, *Reforming Free Will: A Conversation on the History of Reformed Views on Compatibilism (1500–1800)* (Mentor, 2020). I am persuaded by Helm's argument for compatibilism in *Reforming Free Will* (esp. 134–37), which he believes is consistent with Augustine, Turretin, and Edwards. This compatibilism teaches that freedom and responsibility are consistent with determinism.

3. It is important to delineate *human* agency, as there are other moral agents of a different kind, namely angels. The concern of this chapter is not to look at angelic moral responsibility, though we will give brief attention to the deceptive work of Satan.

4. Peter Martyr Vermigli identified this freedom with the image of God and the responsibility of dominion. See Vermigli, *On Free Will and the Law*, in vol. 2 of *A New Translation of the Loci Communes (1576)*, trans. and ed. Joseph A. Tipton (Davenant Press, 2021), 4.

5. Charles Taylor, *The Ethics of Authenticity* (Harvard University Press, 1992), 3.

the *right* action is the *free* action, which is truest to the individual's pursuit of self-fulfillment.[6]

The analysis of the modern moral situation offered by Taylor and others does not identify an entirely new situation but instead an iteration of the moral problem of humanity since Eden. The moral trouble humans have always faced is owing to their (our) denial of the order that is. The precise problem is that humans have demanded to be freed from their place in the given order. But such a demand is an impossibility, as it is a denial of reality. So, the "freedom" humans believe they can/could achieve through the choice of their own order is, in fact, a delusion. Humanity can only ever exist as creatures of the Creator, not as creators of their own reality. Oliver O'Donovan agrees: "The sin by which man has bound himself is the determination to live fantastically, in pursuit of unreality. But freedom can be exercised only in relation to real possibility."[7] The choice to live against God's order is not freedom but enslavement.

The Bible continually speaks of the enslavement of sin because of deception. Nowhere is this made clearer than in Jesus's interaction with the Jews in John 8. In his call to adhere to his word and be his true disciples, he declares that the truth will set a person free (vv. 31–32). The freedom required is deliverance from sin, for "everyone who practices sin is a slave to sin" (v. 34). Jesus elaborates on this point, declaring that opposition to him and his Word is, in fact, opposition to God (vv. 42–43) and the action of children of Satan, the great deceiver in whom there is no truth. Crucially, there is a direct correlation between truth and freedom, deceit and slavery. God speaks the truth, giving the truth in his Word. A denial of the

6. For an extended discussion of this development in modern moral experience, see Taylor, *Ethics of Authenticity*, 1–24. I return to this position, particularly the modern challenge to the community of self-actualization, in chap. 8.

7. Oliver O'Donovan, *Resurrection and Moral Order: An Outline for Evangelical Ethics*, 2nd ed. (Apollos, 1994), 109.

truth is a denial of God himself and of reality itself. Agents operating in denial of the truth are slaves to sin, living lies, choosing what is not good, and following the devil.

Order Overturned: "Did God Really Say . . . ?"

The basic order given in God's good creation is upset in a dramatic way in Genesis 3, leading to cosmological disorder. The opening verse introduces the crafty serpent, clearly classified as a beast of the field. This classification is important as it is a kind (generic) that is ordered *under* the dominion of humanity. The presence of a talking serpent in the garden, along with the historical actuality of a single set of original humans, has troubled many theologians.[8] Personally, I am not troubled by a literal talking serpent, nor of the historical Adam and Eve, for that matter. I am persuaded that the serpent's presence and speech were challenges to the given moral order.[9] Here was an opportunity for humanity to demonstrate obedience to God and acceptance of his ordering of reality. What is most important for our purposes is to acknowledge the moral significance of what is told in the narrative.[10]

The serpent (a beast of the field) comes to tempt the woman to eat fruit (vegetation) in a challenge against the direct command of

8. Surveys of some of these positions may be found in a number of works. See, for example, Matthew Levering, *Engaging the Doctrine of Creation: Cosmos, Creatures, and the Wise and Good Creator* (Baker Academic, 2017), 227–71; Anthony A. Hoekema, *Created in God's Image* (Eerdmans, 1986), 112–32.

9. Kline also notes the significance of *Satan* as the one who assumed the form of a serpent (not indicated in the text, though identified in later texts like Rev. 12:9). Satan, as a fallen angel, was to be judged by humanity, as the apostle Paul would make clear in 1 Cor. 6:2–3. That Adam failed to judge Satan was a failure in his dominion, something for Kline that includes not just the natural created world but also the angelic. Meredith G. Kline, *Kingdom Prologue: Genesis Foundations for a Covenantal Worldview* (Two Age Press, 2000), 121.

10. I believe the *historical* reality of these events is significant for moral reality. As we will see later in this chapter, the transmission of sin begins with our common first parents.

God. Kline notes, "For man to accept the serpent, viewed simply in its animal nature, as his peer, if not superior, among the orders of creation, was to fail to exercise his mandated dominion over the subhuman creatures."[11] What should have been humanity, under God, ruling over animals and plants was instead humanity listening to the animal and making a decision over against God to prize the plant. The order of creation was completely turned upside down.

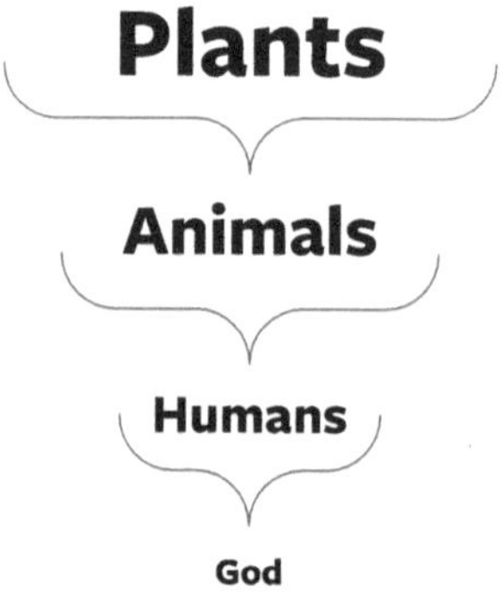

The inverted order of life.

It was this single act against God in Genesis 3 that became not only the real cause of a shift in the cosmos, including the depravity and guilt of all humanity, but also the paradigm of sinful acts. Henceforth, humans will live in denial of a given order, especially God's rule and moral authority. They will, as Romans says, exchange the truth about God for a lie, choosing instead to worship and serve the creature rather than the Creator (Rom. 1:25). This sin will manifest itself in its most overt and grotesque form in idolatrous practices, as well as in its more subversive and sinister forms in egoism and materialism.

11. Kline, *Kingdom Prologue*, 123.

It is important to notice how the initial temptation unfolded and what the first act of rebellion actually was. To be clear, the fruit itself was not bad or evil; therefore, God is not to be blamed for a malignant trap for humanity. The apostle James makes it plain, "Let no one say when he is tempted, 'I am being tempted by God,' for God cannot be tempted with evil, and he himself tempts no one" (James 1:13). The trial of the tree was, in fact, God entrusting creation to the stewardship of humanity within the good order he provided. The command not to eat of *that* tree was a mark of this order. God gave a single opportunity for humanity to submit to his rule.

What, then, was this temptation? In its truest sense, the temptation came from *within* humanity, not without, even if presented by the serpent. The simple question of Genesis 3:1, "Did God actually say . . . ?," raises doubt about the command given by God, both its substance and extent. Eve clarified that the serpent was wrong; God did not prohibit eating from *any* tree, just the *one* tree. But even Eve's clarification is misguided, as she says God prohibited *touching* the tree, not just eating from it. Underlying this initial exchange is a test of understanding the command and the God who delivered it. What *was* the command exactly? Is this *too* strict? Is God *really* good in giving this command? Here, for the first time, Eve must speak of the command from God and give qualifications about it. Dietrich Bonhoeffer sees this moment as the first taste of making judgments against the Word of God: "In this question the possibility is played off against the reality and the possibility undermines the reality. However in man's relationship to God, there are no possibilities, there is only reality."[12]

Turning from the initial question that invited doubt and judgment, the serpent proceeds with an outright lie: "You will not surely die" (Gen. 3:4). This lie is grounded in a reason, casting suspicion on

12. Dietrich Bonhoeffer, *Creation and Fall: A Theological Interpretation of Genesis 1–3* (Macmillan, 1959), 68.

the motive of God's command: "For God knows that when you eat of it your eyes will be opened, and you will be like God, knowing good and evil" (3:5). Here the temptation pushes to the heart of sin, the ego. Pride is what supposedly led to Satan's ruin, and it is pride that led to the ruin of humanity.[13] The reason for choosing to eat the fruit is presented as a means to a better life and existence. The problem, however, is that the promise is of an existence in defiance of order: being *like* God is a promise of equality, something impossible for humankind as a species and a perversion of their proper end.

Sadly, humanity was ruined by conceding to temptation. "So when the woman saw that the tree was good for food, and that it was a delight to the eyes, and that the tree was to be desired to make one wise, she took of its fruit and ate, and she also gave some to her husband who was with her, and he ate" (Gen. 3:6). The *decision* to act in defiance of God's order involved a process. This verse details for us the descent into sin. There was a rationalizing *against* the command from God, grounding the decision in other goods, so the sin was the act in defiance of order. It was a choice for an alternative order, an independent reality, which in the end is unreal. As R. R. Reno says, "Transgression can only allure in a world of distortion and dreamlike fantasy, where what is real becomes malleable, capable of seeming to be what it is not. . . . We can consistently desire what is bad when we imagine that it will add up to something good, a mental operation only possible if we are deceived about reality."[14]

Deception is a matter of knowledge. It issues not from a *lack* of information but from the *mistreatment* of it. This is a consistent point the apostle Paul makes about sin in the Epistle to the Romans.

13. Satan's ruin is nowhere directly detailed in Scripture, but Christian tradition has associated the following texts with the account of Satan's fall: Isa. 14:12; Ezek. 28:13; Job 40:14 (LXX); Ps. 104:26; cf. the apocryphal account in Wis. 2:24. Further, see Augustine, *City of God* 11.15.

14. Reno, *Genesis*, 85.

Knowledge of God is plain enough, evident from the foundation of the world, and therefore humanity is without excuse and justly accountable (Rom. 1:19–20). But unrighteousness is manifest in the suppression of truth (1:18) and in the exchange of the truth of God for a lie (1:25). Because of humanity's mistreatment of truth, God has given humanity over to a "debased mind," leading to further sin as they "do what ought not to be done" (1:28). The corruption of humanity's mind is confirmed later when the apostle calls Christians to transformation through the renewal of their minds (12:2). Interestingly, this transformation—a spiritual work, only in view of the mercies of God (12:1)—leads to discernment of the will of God, "what is good and acceptable and perfect" (12:2). Without this spiritual renewal humanity remains trapped, enslaved to sin, depraved.

Original Sin: The Incapacity and Guilt of All

The total depravity of human beings owes to our progenitor, Adam. Much of the Christian tradition has held a traducian position (that sin is spread *ex traduce*), understanding sin to be transmitted seminally.[15] Historically, this argument has been mounted against Pelagianism.[16] However, this argument predates this theological controversy, as the apostle Paul asserted that "sin came into the world through one man, and death through sin, and so death spread to all men because all sinned" (Rom. 5:12). As the representative of humanity, both

15. This position was held by Augustine, for instance in *City of God* 13.3. It was later embraced by Reformers such as Calvin, in his *Institutes*, 2.1.6–7, and Bullinger, in his *Decades*, 3.10.

16. For instance, this was Augustine's position in much of his writings against Pelagianism. See Augustine, *Anti-Pelagian Writings* (*NPNF*[1], vol. 5) or, specifically, *City of God* 13.3. The Reformers took a similar position, for instance Peter Martyr Vermigli writing against the Pelagian theology of Albert Pighius. See Vermigli, *On Original Sin*, vol. 1 of *A New Translation of the Loci Communes (1576)*, trans. and ed. Kirk Summers (Davenant Press, 2019).

federally and in body, *all* sinned in Adam.[17] When the Reformers expounded Paul's argument, engaging with Pelagianism, it was to argue that salvation is by grace alone, not something we could naturally merit.[18] By nature, we are all "children of wrath" (Eph. 2:3), being dead in our transgressions (2:1).

Paul's argument in Ephesians 2 stood as a landmark text for those combating Pelagianism's contention that humans were born free from sin. The Pelagians contended instead that humans learned to sin through imitation. However, Christian orthodoxy has insisted that the Scriptures plainly teach that human beings are born in sin. David proclaims in Psalm 51:5, "Behold, I was brought forth in iniquity, and in sin did my mother conceive me." Furthermore, many understood Job's question, "Who can bring a clean thing out of an unclean?" (Job 14:4), to reference his being born unclean. Indeed, even from infancy, "none is righteous, no, not one; no one understands; no one seeks for God. All have turned aside; together they have become worthless; no one does good, not even one" (Rom. 3:10–12). Therefore, even from the youngest age, all humanity is guilty of sin.

17. There is a significant theological debate I am not engaging at length here. The traducian view sees a physical link between Adam and his posterity, thus transmitting sin. However, the Reformed traditions are clear that Adam also served as humanity's federal head, representing humanity collectively. I do not believe it is *either* traducian or federal, but both, as many of the Reformers also believed. We are all after Adam, physically, and cursed because of his failure as our federal head. To be freed of the consequences of Adam's sin, we must be born again and united to Christ—the second Adam. For a perspective on sin's corrupting the body and the soul being corrupted through union with the body, and therefore salvation coming to the soul united to Christ and thereby liberating the body from sin, see Vermigli, *On Original Sin*, sections 26–31; 47–51; 55–62; 92–100. One of the significant points of concern for many of the Reformers, following Augustine's argument, was to ensure that there is an understanding of how sin is transmitted, how this doesn't render materiality bad or God at fault, and what it means for the incarnation of Christ.

18. Calvin, *Institutes*, 2.1.7. The Reformers here followed a similar train of thought from Augustine before them (*Enchiridion*, chap. 30)—though this passage engages 2 Pet. 2:19 and John 8:36.

The guilt of infants and young children has stirred up great controversy in the history of discussion about original sin. Why is it that infants should be reckoned guilty as sinners when they have had no opportunity to act? Furthermore, why is it that someone should be punished for the sins of another? Both questions focus on what is meant by Paul when he says, "Therefore, just as sin came into the world through one man, and death through sin, and so death spread to all men because all sinned" (Rom. 5:12). Crucially, what is sin, and what does it mean that all sinned? From this verse (principally) and in answer to this question, the doctrine of original sin is derived.

Original sin stresses the effect of Adam's first sin on humanity after him. The doctrine itself is defined by Peter Martyr Vermigli as "the corrupting of the whole of human nature derived from the fall of the first parent and passed on to posterity through procreation, which, unless the gift of Christ gives aid, sentences all who are born in this state to almost infinite evils and eternal damnation."[19] This historic causal relationship is what Paul discusses in Romans 5. Sin is opposition to the will of God, which Adam performed and which has been passed to his progeny. This means that all in Adam sinned. But humanity's guilt is not for Adam's sin alone, but for our own sinful disposition—our defiance of the will of God. This antagonism springs forth from the deprivation of morality in our nature, the loss of original righteousness. As sin has spread, so too has death. This death is not the fault of Adam alone but is truly the fault of all after Adam because all are born opposed to God.

Concupiscence is the theological term used to depict the opposition of humanity to the will of God. More precisely, it is the "propensity, inclination, natural bent, and proclivity to the doing of evil."[20] Augustine makes it clear that even though parents may be

19. Vermigli, *On Original Sin*, 35.
20. Vermigli, *On Original Sin*, 22.

regenerate, they still conceive children plagued by concupiscence.[21] This is because the birth of children comes by the flesh, whereas spiritual renewal comes by the Spirit. Regeneration is the only means by which someone may be set free from the guilt of concupiscence. Even then, though set free from the bondage of sin, regenerate souls continue to battle the old sinful self. This tension of the old and the new self is captured in many places by the apostle Paul (Rom. 5–8; Gal. 5; Eph. 4:17–5:21; Col. 3:1–17), but perhaps is most clear in his argument in Romans 8:1–17. The life believers now live is in the power of the Spirit. And it is in the Spirit that believers are to put to death the deeds of the flesh. It is, perhaps, the "deeds of the flesh" that most closely correlate with concupiscence because it is the "flesh" that is opposed to God and refuses to submit to God's law (8:7). In fact, "those who are in the flesh cannot please God" (8:8).

The doctrine of total depravity has been central to clear gospel exposition because the flesh is incapable of pleasing God. This doctrine makes it plain why Christ had to redeem humanity. Morally, humans are incapable of doing right (ultimately). Throughout the Epistle to the Romans, Paul uses the word "body" euphemistically to refer to his corrupt nature.[22] He laments, "Wretched man that I am! Who will deliver me from this body of death? (Rom. 7:24). The answer Paul exclaims is, "Thanks be to God through Jesus Christ our Lord!" (7:25). And further, "There is therefore now no condemnation for those who are in Christ Jesus" (8:1). It is only because Christ came in the "likeness of sinful flesh" that he "condemned sin in the flesh" (8:3). Being born of Mary, Christ took a real human nature, though being conceived by the Holy Spirit his nature was free from the

21. Augustine, *A Treatise Concerning Man's Perfection in Righteousness* 2.44 (*NPNF*[1] 5:253).

22. For instance, in Rom. 1:24–25. The consequence of our rejection of God and his ways is a total impact on our lives, experienced through the entirety of our bodily existence. So, when it comes to redemption, we need help with our bodies. See also Rom. 8:13, 22–23; 12:1.

concupiscence the rest of humanity shared through natural generation. And it is only by the Spirit that we can have life in our mortal bodies, which would otherwise remain dead in sin (8:11).

Therefore, because of humanity's depravity, all humans require the work of the Holy Spirit to apply and perfect the work of Christ in them. Truly, "where the Spirit of the Lord is, there is freedom" (2 Cor. 3:17). Thus, people must be "born again" in order to enter the kingdom of God (John 3:3), for "that which is born of the flesh is flesh, and that which is born of the Spirit is spirit" (3:6). Objectively, the law stands over humans condemning them, because subjectively humans oppose the law in their hearts. It is only through the divine work of regeneration that hearts may be turned to the Lord. This is why the Lord promised moral renewal with the coming of his Spirit: "And I will give you a new heart, and a new spirit I will put within you. And I will remove the heart of stone from your flesh and will give you a heart of flesh. And I will put my Spirit within you, and cause you to walk in my statutes and be careful to obey my rules" (Ezek. 36:26–27). It is only when the heart is renewed, when the Spirit issues life, that the mind and will can properly align to the will of God (Rom. 12:2; cf. 1 Cor. 2:6–16).

A Cursed Cosmos

As we move to conclude this brief study of the nature of sin, we should look beyond humanity to the wider effects of sin on the world. In doing so, we begin to perceive how the strife humanity has with the creation issues from the curse. When the order of creation was overturned by Adam (and Eve), the Lord spoke of the consequences of their actions. Their choice against God impacted every facet of life. Rather than upholding and maintaining the order God had provided, they set the creation on a trajectory of disorder of cosmic scale. We'll consider a few ways the kinds of creation were affected, loosely following the order of Genesis 3:14–19, with a view toward broader moral reflection.

First, animals were cursed, impacting their life and their interaction with human beings. This is symbolized in the cursing of the serpent and the enmity God puts between it and the woman and her offspring (Gen. 3:14–15).[23] In the most basic ways, this curse initiates a struggle between beasts and humans. This struggle is not uniform, as the curse itself is not uniform across species, but is total. All are affected, though the serpent is cursed above all others. This cursing of animals explains a great deal of the threat animals pose to human lives, whether it be through poisoning, mauling, or bites. Furthermore, it shows why humans have difficulty taming wild beasts, domesticating them, wrangling, droving, and shepherding them.

Second, human relationships were cursed, impacting their reproduction, domestic interactions, and broader culture (Gen. 3:16). Women will experience pain in childbearing. This is certainly a reference to physical pain and risk associated with pregnancy and birth, but also a reference to the complications faced in procreation more generally (e.g., infertility, loss).[24] The task of procreation will remain, but it will be fraught with pain and challenge. Furthermore, the harmony that husband and wife were to enjoy in their nuptial union will now be complicated by relational strife. Allen P. Ross identifies severe meanings of the words as part of the punishment of sin. The woman's desire would be a "prompting to evil," and the man's "rule" over the woman would be a dominance. So, he concludes, "The woman at her worst would be a nemesis to the man, and the man at his worst would dominate the woman."[25] Thus, ordering in

23. I am making a moral reflection on animals as a kind. This is not the ultimate importance of these verses, as this passage does convey the earliest proclamation of gospel hope. Nonetheless, I do believe that there are significant matters for moral reflection in this text.

24. Ross agrees with this broader reading. See Allen P. Ross, *Creation and Blessing: A Guide to the Study and Exposition of Genesis* (Baker, 1998), 146.

25. Ross, *Creation and Blessing*, 146–47.

the relationship is now difficult. Calvin notes, "She had, indeed, previously been subject to her husband, but that was a liberal and gentle subjection; now, however, she is cast into servitude."[26] Thus, relationships, beginning in the home, are subjected to the curse. These frustrations undoubtedly extend to the wider society.[27] These may not be immediately evident in Genesis 3, but their reach is seen in Genesis 4 as violence spreads: first in Cain killing his brother Abel (4:8), and then in Lamech's murderous vengeance upon a young man (4:23). No longer would human relationships—domestic, social, or political—be without problems.

Third, the ground and vegetation are cursed, impacting agricultural and horticultural work (Gen. 3:17–19). Humanity would continue to cultivate the earth, but it would now be painful and hard labor, and the growth of plants would be riddled with challenges (i.e., thorns and thistles). While this is focused particularly on an agrarian society, work in total is impacted. The earth's environment is hostile to humanity. It is not too much to say that catastrophes such as drought, floods, hurricanes, hail, wildfires, disease, and insect infestations are all evidence of the curse upon the environment. These "natural" disasters are part of the frustration of work brought upon humanity because of their sin.

Finally, the life of human beings is cursed, bringing death. Because humanity chose their own order, they could no longer live, at least not forever. The Lord had purposed to sustain humanity in their existence, providing for them the tree of life in the garden of Eden. But should he permit them to access this tree after the curse, they would be damned to an eternal state of death. Instead, in his great

26. John Calvin, commentary on Genesis 3:16 in vol. 1 of *Calvin's Commentaries* (Baker, 1981).

27. Augustine makes the point that God's ordering of the world was for humanity to have dominion over every irrational creature (i.e., animals), not rational creatures (i.e., humans). *City of God* 19.15.

mercy and kindness, God expelled Adam and Eve from the garden and the tree of life.

Conclusion

It is sobering that the story of the initial disobedience has caused so much disruption and pain. What is more sobering is that this disobedience is in all of us—every human being—as our hearts are set against God. Sin has consequences. The entirety of creation suffers because of humanity's rebellion. As sin is judged, the creation itself must be purged of sin's effects. This was seen in the flood during Noah's time (Gen. 6–9). Then it is warned about in the Prophets, such as the word of the Lord through Zephaniah: "'I will utterly sweep away everything from the face of the earth. . . . I will sweep away man and beast; I will sweep away the birds of the heavens and the fish of the sea, and the rubble with the wicked. I will cut off mankind from the face of the earth,' declares the LORD" (Zeph. 1:2–3). The apostle Peter proclaims, "But the day of the Lord will come like a thief, and then the heavens will pass away with a roar, and the heavenly bodies will be burned up and dissolved, and the earth and the works that are done on it will be exposed" (2 Pet. 3:10). Sin affects everything; therefore, the Lord's coming judgment will be total.

But in his goodness, the Lord also has promised to renew the world. The whole of creation will be restored as sin and evil are judged once and for all. Because sin entered the world through one man, Adam, and death through sin (Rom. 5:12), the Lord graciously sent his Son, the last Adam, to take away the sin of the world (John 1:29) and thereby defeat sin and death and the devil (Heb. 2:14–18). It is in Christ that God has purposed to unite all things (Eph. 1:10), reconciling all things—in heaven and on earth—through the peace won by the blood of the cross (Col. 1:20). And so, not even the worst of moral failures by humanity and the most desperate circumstances under the curse of sin can stop the good plans of God for his creation. He will bring all things to their right end. In fact, even though sin has brought a curse upon the world, God continues to uphold the dignity of humanity after the fall, as we shall consider in the next chapter.

5

Paradise Lost, Dignity Lost?

A Theological Account of Human Worth

> But the primal worthiness cannot come to mind without the sorry spectacle of our foulness and dishonor presenting itself by way of contrast, since in the person of the first man we have fallen from our original condition. From this source arise abhorrence and displeasure with ourselves, as well as true humility; and thence is kindled a new zeal to seek God, in whom each of us may recover those good things which we have utterly and completely lost.[1]
>
> John Calvin

Constructive accounts of human dignity tend to build from either teleological or ontological foundations in the Genesis narrative. But difficulties arise when considering the implications of the fall. Redemption constitutes a certain restoration of dignity. Indeed, Christ himself dignifies humanity. But what of

1. John Calvin, *Institutes of the Christian Religion*, ed. John T. McNeill, trans. Ford Lewis Battles (Westminster, 1960), 2.1.1.

the unregenerate who remain outside of Christ? Is human participation in the created order without good apart from redemption? This chapter seeks a theological locus for human dignity that accounts for the dignity of life for all humans, even after Eden.

There are inherent dangers in this task. I hope to establish human worth for all human beings, regenerate and unregenerate. But dignity and worth are relative concepts.[2] Dignified or honorable before whom? Worth what? Theological orientation locates all things proximate to their God-ordained purpose or ends. But here we find ourselves with a conundrum: If God has purposed all humanity to be rightly ordered to him, how can we call that which is disordered "honorable" or "worthy"? The prophet Malachi gave the rebuke: "You have wearied the LORD with your words. But you say, 'How have we wearied him?' By saying, 'Everyone who does evil is good in the sight of the LORD, and he delights in them'" (Mal. 2:17). I am cautious about calling "good" what the Lord has determined "evil." I wish to delineate between inherent worth/dignity and moral appraisal; I will return to this later in the chapter.

A second danger is that we will have a predetermined conclusion that must find theological justification. For instance, in John F. Kilner's treatise on the image of God, he states, "Considering God's image to be damaged undermines the protections against some of humanity's worst behavior."[3] Kilner's argument here, situated in the broader concepts considered in his work, represents a sentiment that most, if not all, would agree with. There is a fundamental desire to uphold the worth of human life. So, in his treatment, he establishes the preservation of the *imago Dei*, as he sees this as the seat of human

2. For an interesting examination of the differences between dignity and honor in contemporary sociology see Charles Taylor, *The Ethics of Authenticity* (Harvard University Press, 1991), 46–47.

3. John F. Kilner, *Dignity and Destiny: Humanity in the Image of God* (Eerdmans, 2015), 148.

dignity. I do not disagree, but I want to be aware of the danger of predetermined outcomes. What is argued for must be justifiable theologically, not just seen as consequences to avoid in other arguments.

Finally, there is a danger in so wishing to uphold one doctrine that we compromise another, not recognizing unintended consequences. In relation to the present topic, total depravity wrongly conceived of can compromise what God has graciously upheld in humanity even after the fall. Historically, Lutheran theology took a strong turn in this direction, facing controversy over the consequences of the fall and the essence of humanity. This required clarification in the form of the 1577 Solid Declaration of the Formula of Concord (Art. 1: Original Sin). This historical tension relates to a common and abiding question: Has the fall of humanity compromised human dignity? Another way of approaching this question is to ask whether life is worth living for fallen humanity, particularly those who don't know God's redemptive grace.

Though the theme of human dignity is part of a rich and diverse historical conversation, I aim to provide a constructive account of human dignity rather than a work of historical theology. To establish a theological locus for the dignity of all humanity, my argument will proceed as follows. First, I will seek to identify the seat of the *imago Dei*, engaging with ontological and teleological arguments. Second, I will build on recent work in two kingdoms theology to discern the proper assessment of ends—both ultimate and penultimate. Third, I will consider Christ as *the* man, and the relationship of Christology to human dignity. Finally, I will offer conclusions about the noncontingent nature of human worth and God's ultimate purposes, providing a truly theological locus for human dignity.

Ontology and Teleology: Where Do We Locate the *Imago Dei*?

What is it to be human? How are humans distinct from other creatures? In the creation account in Genesis 1:26–28, humanity—both male and female—are created in the image of God. But what this image *is* has been the preoccupation of many through the ages. Broadly speaking, there have been two categories of identification: ontology and teleology. Thorough treatments have been given to these historic positions, so I will only consider the categories broadly.[4]

Ontological arguments have largely identified the image with particular human *faculties*. These faculties have been understood to be the distinctive traits of humanity, setting them apart from the other species in creation. The soul was among the common faculties cited in early patristic theology.[5] Irenaeus considers proper humanity to be a composite of body and soul. "The perfect man consists in the commingling and union of the soul receiving the spirit of the Father, and the admixture of that fleshly nature which was molded after the image of God."[6] Irenaeus expounds this idea, speculating about the possible division of the body and soul. Without the Spirit of God being poured out and blending with the soul, there is only an animal nature that remains and thus an imperfect being, even if the image of God is in some way retained.[7] Augustine builds upon this theology but identifies reason and intellect with the soul. He explains, "God then made man in his own image. For He created for him a soul endowed with reason and intelligence, so that he might excel all the creatures of the earth, air, and sea, which were not so gifted."[8] In the medieval period, Aquinas took a similar line of argument to Augustine but instead emphasized a particular employment of intellect toward the end

4. A few examples of these treatments include: Gerald Bray, "The Significance of God's Image in Man," *Tyndale Bulletin* 42.2 (1991): 195–225; Kilner, *Dignity and Destiny*, 3–51; David H. Kelsey, *Eccentric Existence: A Theological Anthropology*, 2 vols. (Westminster John Knox, 2009); J. Richard Middleton, *The Liberating Image: The* Imago Dei *in Genesis 1* (Brazos, 2005).

5. See, for example, Irenaeus, *Against Heresies* 5.6–7 (*ANF* 1:531–32).

6. Irenaeus, *Against Heresies* 5.6.1.

7. Irenaeus, *Against Heresies* 5.6.1.

8. Augustine, *City of God* 12.23.

of "understanding and loving God."[9] This theology persisted in some form up to the Reformation, as the Reformers sought to understand the consequences of the fall, especially on the will.[10] With this, the Reformers also took notice of character—original righteousness—before the fall, and the derelict character of humanity after the fall.[11]

Teleological arguments, on the other hand, have identified the image of God with particular human *responsibilities*. The cultural mandate in Genesis 1:26b and 1:28—to have dominion, to multiply, to fill the earth and subdue it—is understood to serve as an exposition of what the image is. This ethical component was intended to mirror, or image, the work of God in creation, serving to complete the work that God had begun.[12] Inherent within the teleological arguments is an aversion to ontological issues like the Neoplatonic division of the body and soul often associated with isolation of the faculties.[13] So, Michael Horton says, "Human beings are those who reflect God's image not chiefly in who they *are* essentially but in how they *reply* ethically. Though determined *as* human persons by the mere fact of their creation as God's image, their *realization of the purpose* of their personhood depends on whether they correspond to God's intentions."[14] Those holding a teleological position believe that ontological arguments are static, whereas the biblical witness to humanity's identity is dramatically defined.

The difficulty in exclusively presenting either an ontological or teleological position is that neither accepts an either/or approach. Both see being as something intricately associated with action and

9. Thomas Aquinas, *Summa Theologica* I, q. 93, a. 4.

10. See Calvin, *Institutes*, 2.3.5; Belgic Confession, Art. 14.

11. See Calvin, *Institutes*, 1.15.4; Thirty-Nine Articles of Religion, Arts. 9–10.

12. See David VanDrunen, *Divine Covenants and Moral Order: A Biblical Theology of Natural Law* (Eerdmans, 2014), 61–77.

13. See Michael S. Horton, *Lord and Servant: A Covenant Christology* (Westminster John Knox, 2005), 91–92.

14. Horton, *Lord and Servant*, 97.

purpose. Ontological arguments are not devoid of teleological aims, nor are teleological positions disentangled from ontological facility. Perhaps this tension is where the problem of human dignity is felt most acutely. Can something be if it doesn't act according to its being? Or, to put it another way, is a human truly human if he or she doesn't serve humanity's proper end?

Several recent proposals have examined how being and end fit together in God's design for humanity. Karl Barth, in particular, makes much of God's design for humanity as "covenant partners."[15] He stresses that theological anthropology "asks what kind of a being it is which stands in . . . relationship with God. Its attention is wholly concentrated on this relationship. Thus it does not try to look beyond it or behind it."[16] So, working from a trinitarian analogy in humanity, Barth elevates humanity's capacity for relationship, both as man to God and man to man. Preeminent for Barth was humans' relationship to their fellow man, Jesus Christ, and Christ's relationship to humanity.[17] Wolfhart Pannenberg likewise emphasizes the christological fulfillment of both the ontological and teleological components of the *imago Dei*. He stresses the necessary bifurcation of dignity and destiny for humanity, demanding a historical realization in Christ.[18] For Pannenberg, the great telos of humanity is eternal life in fellowship with God.[19]

Others have recognized God's historical or dramatic intentions in the creation of humanity. That is, humanity was made good, but not perfect (or complete). Early in church history, Irenaeus articulated

15. Karl Barth, *CD*, 14 vols., ed. G. W. Bromiley and T. F. Torrance (Hendrickson, 2004), III/2:319–24.

16. Barth, *CD*, III/2:19. Later Barth wrote, "Theological anthropology must be quite pitiless in its opposition to every attempt to seek real man outside the history of his responsibility to God" (228).

17. Barth, *CD*, III/2:224–28.

18. Wolfhart Pannenberg, *Systematic Theology*, 3 vols. (Eerdmans, 1991), 2:218–31.

19. Pannenberg, *Systematic Theology*, 2:218–31.

the created "imperfection" of humanity, acknowledging that God intended that humanity might grow up into Christ (cf. Eph. 1:10; 4:13–14).[20] This dramatic design has been identified with biblical-theological movements that regard humanity in protological and eschatological terms.[21] Protological humanity was made to reach an eschatological identity.[22] Just as the days were ordered with a Sabbath conclusion, humanity was meant to enter into God's rest (Gen. 2:1–3; Heb. 3:11–4:13). The first Adam (Gen. 1–3; Rom. 5:15–21; 1 Cor. 15:45) was given a theologically ordered task to fulfill in the earth until creation reached its consummation. But in the fall, humans believed a lie and brought disorder in their subversion of God. Consummation was no longer achievable for cursed humanity until Jesus Christ, the second/last Adam (Rom. 5:15–21), took upon himself the likeness of sinful flesh to bring humanity to its proper end (Rom. 8:3–4; 1 Pet. 2:22–25).

We see resonance between the bifurcation of dignity and destiny with the protological and eschatological conceptions of humanity. Rather than jettisoning ontology for teleology, they are held closely together.[23] David VanDrunen writes, "The image, understood in these terms, is not a static ontological reality, but a dynamic, historically/

20. Irenaeus, *Against Heresies* 4.38.

21. VanDrunen identifies three categories: protological image, fallen image, and eschatological image. This correlates with his identification of the *imago Dei* with an ethical response. So the image is kept, but in different form—or better, with different capacity. Sin incapacitates the protological, thus the fallen image, anticipating and looking for *another* to be revealed and enable the eschatological image. See his extensive treatment of these three categories in *Divine Covenants and Moral Order*, 39–94.

22. Geerhardus Vos, *The Eschatology of the Old Testament*, ed. James T. Dennison Jr. (P&R, 2001), 73–76. See also William Dumbrell, *The Search for Order: Biblical Eschatology in Focus* (Baker, 1994), 21–22.

23. Kapic, for example, is wary of identifying the image with either faculties (ontology) or relationship (teleology), and instead chooses a both/and. Kelly M. Kapic, "Anthropology," in *Christian Dogmatics: Reformed Theology for the Catholic Church*, ed. Michael Allen and Scott R. Swain (Baker Academic, 2016), 170. This is in contrast to Horton, who sees the image as "ethical rather than ontological" (*Lord and Servant*, 112).

teleologically/eschatologically oriented office that entails being equipped for a task, performing the task, and attaining the goal."[24] Considering sin, we see the failure of reaching a telos and therefore must ask whether this compromises identity and dignity.

In anticipation of the conclusions of this chapter, I wish to affirm that dignity is an indelible characteristic belonging to all human persons. Dignity is tied to the irrevocable *imago Dei*. This recognizes the intimate connection of ontology and teleology but does not deny the ontological when the teleological is compromised (Gen. 9:1–8; Rom. 1:18; James 3:9). To make this point, Reinhold Niebuhr uses the analogy of an eye, recognizing that just because an eye goes blind it does not change the essence of the eye.[25] Likewise, Barth affirms, "The ontological band which binds every man to God is the honour which God shows him, even if he is a theoretical and practical atheist, in the fact that He is always his Creator and Lord, so that he for his part, however well or badly, was and is and will be His creature."[26] Human dignity cannot be lost.

The dignifying characteristic of humanity, then, is not the active participation of humanity according to our identity in the image of God, but instead in God's benevolent upholding of humanity as his creatures. This involves capacity (ontology) for covenant partnership (relationship/ethics/telos), but human dignity is not contingent on right human action or retained capacity; dignity is by divine bestowal, by the relationship of the Creator to his creatures. In fact, the capacity for covenant partnership is something for which humanity is held

24. VanDrunen, *Divine Covenants and Moral Order*, 40. I cite VanDrunen here in support of my argument, though he himself supports a teleological/ethical account of the *imago Dei*. I have taken this liberty because I believe that his argument reinforces my point that the ontological and teleological are mutually dependent. So here, he identifies ontological equipment for an ethical task.

25. Reinhold Niebuhr, *The Nature and Destiny of Man: A Christian Interpretation*, one-volume ed. (Scribner's Sons, 1949), 266–67.

26. Barth, *CD*, III/4:652.

to account by God at the final judgment (eschatologically); as such, accountability serves as a mark of dignity, demonstrating the regard of the Creator for humanity.[27] As the psalmist says, "What is man that you are mindful of him, and the son of man that you care for him? Yet you have made him a little lower than the heavenly beings and crowned him with glory and honor. You have given him dominion over the works of your hands; you have put all things under his feet" (Ps. 8:4–6).

If, as I have argued, dignity in humanity is divinely ascribed, this means that dignity is not self-determined. It is found both in knowing what we are and what we are for, as what we are accords with what we are for. John Webster states, "In the matter of human dignity, there is no absolutely original self-knowledge; creaturely self-knowledge is a creaturely act, and therefore an act whose description requires talk of God the creator."[28] Human *creatureliness* is where dignity is found.[29] In Genesis 1:27, man and woman are both created in God's image. After the fall, God sent Adam and Eve away from the garden but permitted their ongoing existence (Gen. 3:22–24). After humanity's depravity reached an intolerable peak that demanded immediate justice through judgment (Gen. 6:5–7, 11–12, 17), God preserved righteous Noah through the flood (Gen. 6:8–9, 18–22). After the flood, God recommissioned Noah with a reiteration of the culture mandate (in modified form), once more recognizing that humanity is to be rightly regarded because they bear the image of God.[30] The climax of human history and the ultimate affirmation of human honor is the eternal Son becoming incarnate, in order to provide for humanity all that is necessary to live as true humans (Heb. 2:5–18).

27. John Webster, "The Dignity of Creatures," in vol. 2 of *God Without Measure: Working Papers in Christian Theology* (T&T Clark, 2015), 37.

28. Webster, "Dignity of Creatures," 33.

29. Webster, "Dignity of Creatures," 30, 34.

30. For an interesting and helpful discussion of the Noahic covenant, including remarks on the *lex talionis*, see VanDrunen, *Divine Covenants and Moral Order*, 95–132.

So, human dignity is common in the prelapsarian and postlapsarian world. However, though dignity is upheld, I do *not* want to overlook important movements in history, as if the human condition is static. We must explore the relationship of human dignity to both sin on the one hand and the person and work of Christ on the other.

Moral Assessment

How are we to account for sin with respect to the dignity of humanity? Put simply, sin is a denial of what *is*. Webster defines sin as "disobedience, lack of assent to that which has been given to the creature as the shape of being, and so a contradiction of creatureliness (in Augustine's terms, a descent to the bestial). As such, it is a worthless attack on both God's honor and on the honor of creatures. In withholding compliance to the being and destiny of creatures, it erodes creaturely dignity."[31] But no matter how much a human denies what he or she is—a creature accountable to the Creator—a human cannot change his or her status as a creature: a human. As Barth says, "Even as a sinner he [man] remains the creature of God and therefore the being whose orientation is to be the covenant-partner of God. He can give himself up for the lost. But he cannot escape God, or lose his being as the creature of God, or the nature of this being."[32] Sin, therefore, does not take away from human dignity but instead is a denial of the dignified existence granted by the grace of God. So, while humans do not change their being in sin, they can deny their proper telos in sin. Thus, it can be said that all life has dignity, but not all living is dignified. It is the notion of dignified living that leads us to the relationship between moral assessment and human worth.

31. Webster, "Dignity of Creatures," 39.
32. Barth, *CD*, III/2:319.

Though human dignity is preserved through the fall, sin is not without consequence. Judgment for sin is and will be rendered. Temporally, humanity experiences the immediate consequences of sin through the dissatisfaction and disorder of life lived in misdirection. Pannenberg explains, "Misery, then, is the lot of those who are deprived of the fellowship with God that is the destiny of human life. Alienation from this destiny does not abolish it. Its continued presence is the basis of our misery, for in alienation from God we are robbed of our true identity."[33] Of course this misery is not always recognized existentially. Malachi's caution against the prophets calling "good" what is "evil" was based on their perception that God did not and would not judge; instead, they observed that the wicked prospered in their embrace of immorality (Mal. 2:17; 3:13–14). But though temporal judgment may not be recognized, eschatological judgment is sure (Mal. 3:16–4:3; Rev. 19:1–3). The greatest atrocity implied in Malachi's warning is not that the sinners kept sinning, as terrible as this is, but that they thought God is unjust. Their theology was false and so they lived accordingly.

Moral judgment seemingly implies multiple ends: the righteous to the inheritance of eternal life, the wicked to eternal damnation (Matt. 25; Rev. 20:11–15). There is a tendency for theological assessments of humanity to seek an eschatological judgment only (synchronic), perhaps at the exclusion of God's providence in time (diachronic). The dignity of the reprobate must be held in tension with their ultimate judgment. Scripture upholds this tension in passages such as Psalm 145:14–20:

> The LORD upholds all who are falling
> and raises up all who are bowed down.
> The eyes of all look to you,
> and you give them their food in due season.

33. Pannenberg, *Systematic Theology*, 2:179.

You open your hand;
 you satisfy the desire of every living thing.
The LORD is righteous in all his ways
 and kind in all his works.
The LORD is near to all who call on him,
 to all who call on him in truth.
He fulfills the desire of those who fear him;
 he also hears their cry and saves them.
The LORD preserves all who love him,
 but all the wicked he will destroy.

God's common provision extends universally to all humanity (vv. 14–17). Yet, there is particular provision for those of the redeemed community: the satisfaction of fellowship with God, as he is properly revered (vv. 18–19). Ultimately, eschatologically, there is judgment where the redeemed are preserved and the wicked destroyed (v. 20). Yet, notice the two kinds of satisfaction to be found in humanity: *Commonly* the Lord satisfies "the desire of every living thing," but *particularly* he fulfills the desire of those who fear him. Here we see what appear to be two different ends.[34]

The recognition of the common and the particular has been articulated most helpfully within two kingdoms theology.[35] David VanDrunen identifies how God's preservation of the world permits service of both ultimate and penultimate ends.[36] So, the com-

34. I am arguing here from a classic position that desires accord with ends. See Aristotle, *Nicomachean Ethics,* ed. Lesley Brown, trans. David Ross, Oxford World's Classics (Oxford University Press, 2009), 1.7.

35. David VanDrunen has undertaken this project most prolifically, though he is not alone. Some recent works include VanDrunen, *Natural Law and the Two Kingdoms: A Study in the Development of Reformed Social Thought* (Eerdmans, 2010); VanDrunen, *Divine Covenants and Moral Order*; VanDrunen, *Politics After Christendom: Political Theology in a Fractured World* (Zondervan Academic, 2020); VanDrunen, *Living in God's Two Kingdoms: A Biblical Vision for Christianity and Culture* (Crossway, 2010).

36. David VanDrunen, "The Importance of the Penultimate: Reformed Social Thought and the Contemporary Critiques of the Liberal Society," in *Journal of Markets & Morality* 9, no. 2 (Fall 2006): 219–49.

mon (civil) kingdom serves penultimate or temporal purposes, whereas the redemptive (spiritual) kingdom serves ultimate or eschatological ends. These kingdoms are not separated, but in some ways are integrated.[37] That is, the common and the redemptive interact, and God is sovereign over all. The common kingdom enjoys God's prudential plan for his creation, most clearly articulated in his covenant with Noah. In Genesis 9:1–17, God upholds certain temporal goods for creation in a postlapsarian world.[38] Notice that this is not salvific provision. The redemptive kingdom enjoys God's eschatological plan for his creation, promised in the covenant of grace for salvation.

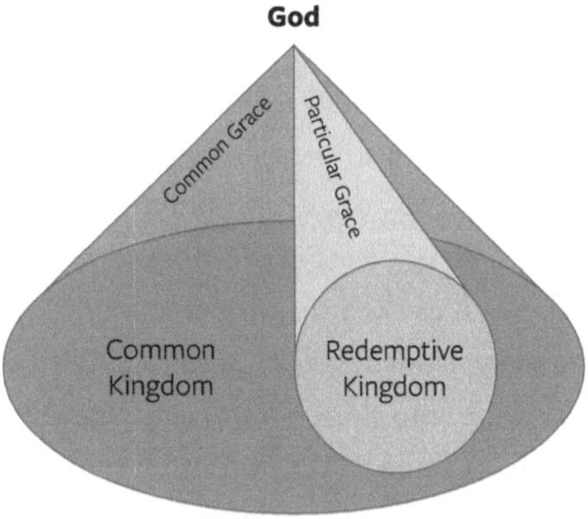

Two kingdoms and grace.

So, what belongs to the common kingdom is truly common, belonging to all, while the redemptive kingdom is particular to God's

37. Pannenberg helpfully corrected misconceptions related to Luther's theology of the two kingdoms, noting that Luther did not believe that the kingdom of God and the kingdom of the world were completely separate. Wolfhart Pannenberg, *Ethics*, trans. Keith Crim (Westminster, 1981), 112–31.

38. Pannenberg, *Ethics*, 233.

elect. Key to the distinction of penultimate and ultimate ends is the achievement of Christ in relationship to the mandate given to humanity at creation. After the fall, humanity cannot achieve the consummation of the new creation; this work belongs to Christ alone. Political and cultural participation in society is still worthwhile following the fall, but it should be understood as God's plan for sustaining his world, *not* redeeming it.[39]

Of Christ and Human Worth

Having seen that salvation and the new creation come through Christ alone, we must now consider how the person and work of Christ specifically relate to the dignity of humanity. The eternal Son comes as a man, not just *in* the image of God but *as* the image of God (Col. 1:15–20; Heb. 1:3–4; 2:5–9). In this way, Christ serves as *the* man, Adam par excellence. However, in Colossians 1, there is another sense that this is also qualified by works seemingly resonant with Adam's original mandate, such as creation, dominion, and multiplication. Christ fulfills these all as the preeminent One. Kelly Kapic puts it well: "This last Adam is not a picture of some primitive human creature but rather the one who alone is able to serve as the representative for humanity who consummates its purpose. Coming, as it were from the future, the last Adam breaks into the present to give humanity a taste of the expected shalom and to hold it secure in that reality even before it has yet been fully realized."[40] Christ's incarnation serves to bring humanity to its proper end, and this eschatological work

39. Calvin, *Institutes*, 2.3.4. This stands in distinct contrast to the transformationist eschatology of scholars like Wolters and Wright. See Albert M. Wolters, *Creation Regained: Biblical Basics for a Reformational Worldview*, 2nd ed. (Eerdmans, 2005); N. T. Wright, *Surprised by Hope: Rethinking Heaven, the Resurrection, and the Mission of the Church* (Harper One, 2008).

40. Kapic, "Anthropology," 180.

is breaking into the present world by the work of the Holy Spirit, uniting the redeemed to Christ.

The salvific achievement of Christ, therefore, required an incarnate existence. Christ came as our brother, in flesh and blood, in ontological solidarity with us (Heb. 2:5–18). His incarnation reveals that sin is not something belonging to the essence of human being, as Christ is sinless, although there is a clear acknowledgment that Christ came in the likeness of sinful flesh (Rom. 8:3). This is to say that Christ came in very real human existence, a cursed existence, with all of its depraved desires, yet without sin. So, he achieved what no other could.

It was because of his ontological solidarity with us as a true human that Christ could achieve humanity's proper end. This involved him recapitulating both Adam's and Israel's history. In doing so, Jesus did not bring us back to a state of original innocence but takes us forward to eschatological achievement: the consummation of a new creation in glory.[41] Jesus does not call humanity back to Adam's original mandate; he beckons humanity to rest in his finished work. In spiritual union with him, he enables humanity to enjoy proper fellowship with God as well as communion with fellow human beings.

It is, therefore, appropriate to say that Christ restored dignity to humanity in a very real sense. Human dignity is undeniable among all of humanity because humans are creatures of God. Yet it is only because the Creator became a creature that creatures can reach their proper end. The tragedy of the incarnation was that "he was in the world, and the world was made through him, yet the world did not know him. He came to his own, and his own people did not receive him" (John 1:10–11). But the promise held out to humanity is that "to all who did receive him, who believed in his name, he gave the right to become children of God, who were born, not of blood nor of the will of the flesh nor of the will of man, but of God" (1:12–13).

41. Horton, *Lord and Servant*, 220.

The achievement of Christ is only known to us now in part as we await the final consummation. This means that redeemed humanity continues to cohabitate with common humanity, both dignified, but with different ends. The common kingdom (in which all humanity participates) serves penultimate ends of preservation while this world endures (Gen. 8:22). The redemptive kingdom awaits its consummation. The consummation will not come as a result of the efforts of the redeemed in any social or political context. Rather, the redeemed tell of the Redeemer (Matt. 24:14), beckoning fellow humans to come to the place where they can reach their ultimate purpose of knowing the Father, through the Son, in the Spirit, delighting in communion with God and his people.

Conclusion

Throughout this chapter, I have argued that humanity is universally dignified, not because of self-appraisal but because of divine bestowal. As creatures of the Creator there is an inherent dignity of being regarded by God Almighty, even as accountable to him. Human dignity, then, is a unidirectional status. It cannot be revoked, because God does not cease to consider his creation. Thus, worth is *not* contingent on human performance. Saying so would render all unredeemed humanity worthless. It also would compromise the very grace of the gospel, which demonstrates that "while we were still sinners, Christ died for us" (Rom. 5:8). More than mere creational status (but certainly not less than), human dignity is demonstrated in Christ's salvific work for the unrighteous.

Though dignity is not contingent upon human performance, humans can live undignified lives. That is, they can live *unhuman* lives, both in denial of their true identity and the identity of others. Denying divinely ordered existence is a denial of reality. The more that humans deny proper relationship to God as their sovereign, proper relationship with other human beings as image bearers, and proper relationship with the rest of creation over which they've been given stewardship, the more they live an undignified existence. Life won't be worthless because God upholds his regard for humanity, but human existence will be increasingly frustrated and dissatisfying. God preserves particular goods for humanity in creation, but without proper orientation to God in Christ, these will ultimately be condemned.

I have mentioned the ultimate end of humanity, of which the Westminster Catechism is surely correct to say is glorifying God and enjoying him forever (Question 1). But what of God? Humanity's ultimate end correlates with God's, for it is divinely determined. Though humanity may fail in reaching their ultimate end apart from divine intervention, God will never fail in reaching his. God's glory is not contingent upon humanity's performance or proper recognition of him. So, while humanity's purpose is to know and enjoy God in glorious communion, their failure will not compromise God's glory. "This is what the LORD has said: 'Among those who are near me I will be sanctified, and before all the people I will be glorified'" (Lev. 10:3). Elsewhere, God declares, "I am the LORD; that is my name; my glory I give to no other, nor my praise to carved idols" (Isa. 42:8). The Lord will be glorified as he brings all things to their proper end at the eschaton: the redeemed to the glory of the new creation, the reprobate to their destruction. But even this reckoning will be a demonstration of God's regard for humanity.

The tragedy of humanity is its denial of its Creator. This is sinfulness. However, though humanity may wish to deny its chief end, it cannot escape the question of its chief end. What are people for? O'Donovan insists, "Without some answer to that question it has lost, not only the grounds for respecting this human species (thus leaving itself engaged upon a pointless self-worship), but also . . . the very reason to understand humanity as a unitary species at all, rather than as a chance objectification, or 'tragic thrownness,' of being."[42] Without knowing what humanity is for (teleologically), humanity cannot know what it is (ontologically). A right appreciation of humanity takes into account that God creates all human beings in his image, dignified *beings* with a glorious *purpose*. In the next chapter, we will examine how humanity, both redeemed and unredeemed, know the moral order and interact with the knowledge they have, and we'll ask why all will be held morally accountable.

42. Oliver O'Donovan, *Resurrection and Moral Order: An Outline for Evangelical Ethics*, 2nd ed. (Eerdmans, 1994), 37–38.

6

Knowledge and Moral Authority

> We are . . . reminded that the only rule for acting well is, to undertake nothing but by the direction and commandment of God. And if after this the whole world should rise against us, we shall still have this invincible defence, that he who follows God cannot go astray.[1]
>
> John Calvin

A COMMON THEOLOGICAL GROWTH PERIOD IN the Christian life tends to occur during adolescence. For some reason, it is the teenage years when questions about God's election, or predestination, emerge. Young people begin to grasp the significance of sin and the implications this has for knowing and willing. As they discover that humans can only turn to God because he has first worked in them, they question the justness of this reality. Accompanying this concern, they wonder about universal accountability: Why should people be held responsible for something they are not free to turn

1. John Calvin, *Commentary on the Gospel According to John*, in *Calvin's Commentaries* (Baker, 1991), 18:211–12.

away from? These questions are not unique to young adults. Questions may begin early, but they haunt thoughtful people throughout their lives as they witness many people dear to them remain in sin and live in active denial of their Creator.

In this chapter, I do not seek to answer all the questions people have concerning election—a difficult but beautiful doctrine. Instead, I will pursue this tension in view of ethics. How do humans access knowledge of what is good? How does access impact accountability? I will consider how the challenge of faith is now complicated by the noetic effects of the fall. In our desire as humans to *decide* right and wrong, we have been cursed not actually to know right from wrong in an ultimate sense. Though the curse is pervasive, we are not without God's gracious provision. Following the four laws of Thomas Aquinas (eternal, divine, natural, and human) and their reception among the Reformed Orthodox, I examine what moral knowledge can be known and by whom. Building upon a rich tradition, I explore how two kingdoms theology aligns with this moral knowledge and provides a model for political participation. I hope to demonstrate that God's law establishes ethical reality and is known in various ways based on the administration of grace.

The Noetic Effects of Sin

In the previous chapter, I examined original sin's effect on humanity's corruption and guilt. Here, I do not wish to restate that point but simply to consider the effect of total depravity on the intellect. How has sin corrupted knowledge? Answering this question will better position us to grasp what access humanity has to ethical information and their ability to live morally. In short, my argument is that all humanity has been impacted by original sin and, therefore, cannot live a righteous life apart from divine intervention. However, though there is universal guilt and the noetic effects of sin extend to all, there remains just moral accountability for all.

In addition to what Romans 1 says about the impact of sin upon the mind, Ephesians 4 provides further evidence of the noetic effects of sin. The apostle Paul challenges the Ephesian believers to no longer live like the Gentile unbelievers but instead to realize the transformation of new life in gospel faith. The Gentiles live according to the "futility of their minds" because they are "darkened in their understanding, alienated from the life of God because of the ignorance that is in them, due to their hardness of heart" (4:17–18). Before life in Christ, there is no knowing God's ways, and this ignorance is owing to a spiritual condition. Depravity abounds, trapping people in their rebellion against God. Calvin infers from these verses that "the grace of Christ is the sole remedy to free us from that blindness and from the evils consequent upon it."[2] Calvin agrees with Augustine on the noetic effects of sin, stating that "the will is indeed free but not freed: free of righteousness but enslaved to sin!"[3]

Arguing against the Pelagian heresy, Augustine contends that humanity is free and yet is unable to do good apart from the grace of God.[4] On freedom, he argues that God's commands would be useless if they were unable to be performed, and they are given so that ignorance may not be claimed as an excuse.[5] Furthermore, ignorance is not a valid excuse, even if ignorance (genuine, not unwilling) may suffer a lesser consequence.[6] In this way, Augustine stresses the heightened moral responsibility of those who have been told God's ways (cf. Rom. 2). Finally, concupiscence is also not an excuse for inability or lack of knowledge because it is proof of evil within and failure to consent to God's righteous commands.[7] The power to know good

2. John Calvin, *Institutes of the Christian Religion*, ed. John T. McNeill, trans. Ford Lewis Battles (Westminster, 1960), 2.3.1.

3. See Calvin, *Institutes*, 2.2.8, where he expounds Augustine's doctrine of "free will."

4. Augustine, "On Grace and Free Will" (*NPNF*[1] 5:443–65).

5. Augustine, "On Grace and Free Will," chaps. 2–4.

6. Augustine is adamant that no excuse will exempt a sinner from the punishment of eternal fire (i.e., hell). Augustine, "On Grace and Free Will," chap. 5.

7. Augustine, "On Grace and Free Will," chap. 5.

and to will and act in accordance with the good is only possible by divine grace.[8] Both justification and transformation of believers, and all the good merits they begin to show henceforth, must be attributed to God's grace.[9]

Perhaps one of the clearest synopses of the relationship between the will and the state of humanity under sin is found in Petrus van Mastricht's work.[10] He explores the will morally, identifying the fourfold good and fourfold state of humanity. For good, there is the natural good (e.g., eating, drinking, speaking), the civil good (e.g., kindness to one's neighbor, refraining from violence), the moral or ecclesial good (e.g., prayers, abstaining from offenses), and the spiritual or saving good (e.g., faith, hope). From this fourfold good, Mastricht explores which good could be known and chosen in the fourfold state of humanity. The state of integrity was the initial state of humanity (prelapsarian) when there was a choice of good and evil. The state of sin permits a choice of natural, civil, or moral good. The state of grace allows the choice of any good or evil. And in the state of glory, there is only a choice of good. Mastricht provides the following summary: "Liberty does survive in our choice, even after sin, a liberty that is essential to man's nature, one by which all the worst men, whatever they do, do it freely; yet not such a liberty as is independent from the first cause, nor which is fitted with the strength for spiritual good, to accomplish it spiritually, and in this respect it is rather called enslaved than free."[11]

8. Augustine, "On Grace and Free Will," chap. 6, 446.

9. Augustine, "On Grace and Free Will," chap. 13, 449.

10. Petrus van Mastricht, *The Works of God and the Fall of Man*, vol. 3 of *Theoretical-Practical Theology*, ed. Joel R. Beeke, trans. Todd M. Rester (Reformation Heritage, 2021), 527. What follows is a summary of the argument from this section.

11. Mastricht, *Works of God*, 527. Elsewhere Mastricht provides a similar reflection on mankind's moral need for God: "Not only does the intellect of the person to be converted labor under its own blindness, but also the will, under its aversion from God and every spiritual good, and under a propensity toward contrary things; accordingly,

In this brief consideration of the noetic effects of sin—beginning with Scripture's testimony in the writing of the apostle Paul, through the theological studies of Augustine, Calvin, and Mastricht—we've seen that there is a simultaneous freedom and enslavement. Humankind makes genuine choices that may be called free, but these choices are not free for choosing righteousness. Humankind is only righteous by the grace of God. This does not cancel moral accountability but grounds our accountability in that universal human identity in Adam, our progenitor, in whom we all sinned (Rom. 5:12–13). I began this chapter with the question of the justice of moral accountability where there is a lack of knowledge or ability. In the remainder of the chapter, I will consider how God has graciously enabled and preserved knowledge of the moral order and enabled moral action, even penultimately good action, as part of his plans for the world.

Before we proceed, it is important to note something I've been assuming thus far about the nature of what can be known morally and how it relates to the will. Throughout the book, I have been contending for moral realism, something that Rufus Black notes is "the ultimate epistemological grounding for moral truth is a given reality external to the will."[12] I have been contending that goodness is objective, not something determined volitionally. To contend otherwise equates what is good with what is chosen—something I've noted amongst contemporary ethical pursuits. But in contradistinction to this subjective position, which finds its expression so often in expressive individualism and even in more corporate utilitarian ethics, theology demands an objective morality. Participation in the world is participation in a given order of being, a moral reality beyond the subject. To recognize this reality "is to discover the character

this necessarily requires that by the physical operation of God there be removed not only blindness from the intellect, but also that corruption from the will." *Works of God*, 361.

12. Rufus Black, *Christian Moral Realism: Natural Law, Narrative, Virtue, and the Gospel* (Oxford University Press, 2000), 8.

of the moral order as *authority*, and so to establish that authority is the objective correlation of freedom."[13] True freedom is not living according to subjective determination but discovering the objective order and aligning with that way of being. As I've argued, this order is divinely determined and revealed distinctly in different domains. Each account of law coheres with and relates to a universal order for the cosmos—the exception being human law, which is a societal approximation of the good.[14]

Ultimate Reality: Eternal Law

For Aquinas, law serves as the basic principle of human operations, ruling and measuring acts.[15] He believes that human reason enables the discernment of law, distinguishing humans as moral beings over against animals. As in so many other philosophical matters, Aquinas follows Aristotle in noting law as a principle of reason, which necessarily must principally regard its last end. This end he identifies as bliss or happiness. So, he argues, law must serve this highest end.[16]

The triune God exists in eternal bliss. This is not a static reality, but one of active relational delight between Father, Son, and Holy Spirit. Describing this reality, we might say that God acts according to an eternal law—one that precedes time and is not subject to time.[17] This law is not a formula separate from God's being but instead a

13. Oliver O'Donovan, "What Can Ethics Know About God?," in *The Doctrine of God and Theological Ethics*, ed. Alan J. Torrance and Michael Banner (T&T Clark, 2006), 39–40.

14. O'Donovan notes that many of the historical accounts of law configured public authority as an extension of God's law. This certainly could be said to be true of Aquinas and Richard Hooker. In this view, human law was supported as part of God's authority over the world. Oliver O'Donovan, *The Desire of the Nations: Rediscovering the Roots of Political Theology* (Cambridge University Press, 1996), 234.

15. Aquinas, *Summa Theologica* I-II, q. 90, a. 1.

16. Aquinas, *Summa Theologica* I-II, q. 90, a. 2.

17. Aquinas, *Summa Theologica* I-II, q. 91, a. 1

description of God's perfect being in action. In one sense, this law is the highest good—the chief end (telos) of all that is. So, the eternal law is, in effect, that God himself is the highest good, and in him is infinite delight. God's activity is according to his being, so God is good, God is love, and so on. If we could specify "reason" within God's existence, it would be the eternal reason to act according to his being, which is the chief end of all action. Crucially, when God acts beyond himself—his transitive acts (*ad extra*)—he creates an order according to this eternal law. In other words, God's creation is properly ordered toward God as its chief end.

God alone can know the eternal being and activity of the Godhead without mediation. Creatures, however, *do* know something of the eternal law, says Aquinas, through participation. God is the rule maker, knowing the rule in his own being, but we creatures are ruled and measured by God's rule. In other words, God is the artificer and creation presents an imprint of his eternal law as artifacts. The created order tells something of its Maker. We know the effects of the eternal law in the way that "someone not seeing the sun in its substance, may know it by its rays."[18] Only God knows the eternal law, though something of the fullness of this law will be known at the end of time when the righteous will behold God.[19] This will be the state of glory Mastricht refers to, in which there will only be a choice of good.

Two Kingdoms

As we consider God's revelation of moral order in the creation, let us return to the two kingdoms theology I began exploring in the last chapter. As noted there, David VanDrunen has ably retrieved

18. Aquinas, *Summa Theologica* I-II, q. 93, a. 2.

19. Aquinas believed that "final and perfect happiness can consist in nothing else than the vision of the Divine Essence." *Summa Theologica* I-II, q. 3, a. 8. I will consider the beatific vision in chap. 9.

and espoused this theology in his recent works.[20] Here, my concern is not to justify this theology or offer an extensive treatment but instead to show how the two kingdoms relate to God's moral order and the revelation he provides. In short, there is a direct correlation between what is revealed of the moral order through natural law and the common (or civil) kingdom and what is revealed through divine law and the redemptive (or spiritual) kingdom.

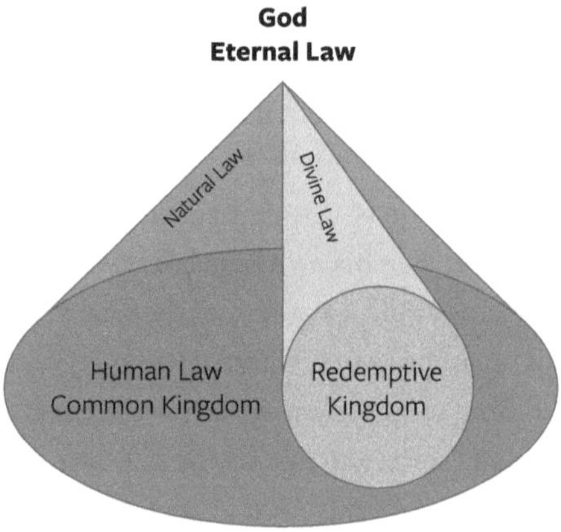

Two kingdoms and law.

The civil kingdom is the *universal* or common domain over which Christ rules providentially as provider and sustainer, upholding

20. VanDrunen produced a trilogy covering different aspects of natural law in relation to the two kingdoms: *Natural Law and the Two Kingdoms: A Study in the Development of Reformed Social Thought* (Eerdmans, 2010); *Divine Covenants and Moral Order: A Biblical Theology of Natural Law* (Eerdmans, 2014); and *Politics After Christendom: Political Theology in a Fractured World* (Zondervan Academic, 2020). Beyond these academic volumes, VanDrunen has also ventured to make aspects of two kingdoms theology more widely accessible in several introductory volumes: *Living in God's Two Kingdoms: A Biblical Vision for Christianity and Culture* (Crossway, 2010); and *Natural Law: A Short Companion*, Essentials in Christian Ethics, ed. C. Ben Mitchell and Jason Thacker (B&H Academic, 2023). What I explain of two kingdoms theology in this chapter is indebted to what I have learned from VanDrunen.

goodness for penultimate ends. The spiritual kingdom is the *particular* domain over which Christ rules salvifically as Redeemer unto ultimate ends.[21]

Based on what we have seen of the noetic effects of sin, it is important to note that the preservation of the world and human life, including moral order after the fall, are all owing to God's grace. Returning to our initial question of justice, it is merciful that God permits humans to live life when they rebel as creatures against their Creator. We may recall the benevolence seen in Psalm 145: "The Lord is good to all, and his mercy is over all that he has made" (v. 9). He continues to sustain life, satisfying the desires of every living thing (v. 16). All may be satisfied penultimately, but the Lord ultimately fulfills the desires of those who fear him (v. 19). And so, we attribute God's merciful sustenance of the world to his grace. We speak of God's common grace for those provided for in a temporal (penultimate) way. We speak of God's particular or redeeming grace for those provided for in an eternal (ultimate) way.

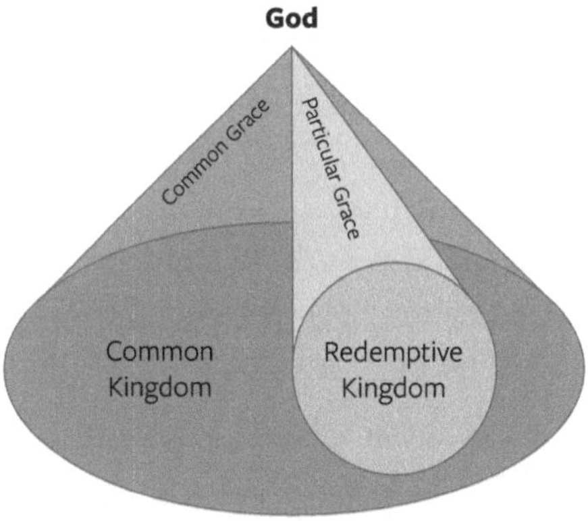

Two kingdoms and grace.

21. VanDrunen, *Natural Law and the Two Kingdoms*, 1–2.

Some have taken issue with two kingdoms theology, seeing it as an inadequate biblical and theological vision for public theology. Dan Strange, for example, has quipped that a vision for natural law grounded in natural revelation dismisses the sufficiency of Scripture.[22] Likewise, James K. A. Smith has critiqued the position, saying that it overlooks the "liturgical" nature of all of life and arguing idolatry is the problem with the world.[23] These critiques propose a more holistic vision for a single ethical demand on the world. But both critiques fail to recognize that the division of kingdoms isn't a division of morality per se, proposing distinct moral realities. Instead, two kingdoms theology proposes a distinction of expectations. The two kingdoms' moral order agrees, but each kingdom's ends are discreet: The civil kingdom will only ever know morality naturally and thereby only live unto penultimate ends; the spiritual kingdom will know morality through divine special revelation and will thereby live unto an ultimate end. This does not mean that there are separate moral orders; instead, epistemological differences correlate with different ends.[24]

Providence: Common Grace for the Common Kingdom

The civil kingdom is the domain that encompasses all human life in the world. For this kingdom, God provides common grace to sustain the world unto penultimate ends, enabling life to persist, societies to develop, and temporal justice to be administered. This kingdom provides the stage of history for the gospel to advance. Were God to bring

22. Dan Strange, "Not Ashamed! The Sufficiency of Scripture for Public Theology," *Themelios* 36, no. 2 (2011): 238–60.

23. James K. A. Smith, "Reforming Public Theology: Two Kingdoms, or Two Cities?," *Calvin Theological Journal* 47 (2012): 122–37.

24. It does not appear that Smith or Strange have clearly grasped the vision set forward in VanDrunen's work, often overlooking crucial sections of engagement that answer specifically the questions they raise. They settle for caricatures of the position, such as calling VanDrunen's position one that sees Scripture in some way insufficient(!).

the cosmos to its ultimate end, all that is not properly ordered unto him would perish. So, the civil kingdom is God's merciful provision for the world to persist despite its rebellion against his ultimate order. Moral knowledge in this domain is given through natural law and is sufficient for penultimate goods.[25] This knowledge serves as the basis for formulating human law governing relationships between humans.

Knowing Through General Revelation: Natural Law

Natural law is the law God has provided to all humanity in the created order, known through human faculties of sense perception, conscience, and intellect (i.e., rationality).[26] Aquinas offers a thorough discourse on natural law in his Treatise on Law, from which many Reformed scholars advanced a similar theology.[27] He contends that humans maintain rationality as part of their being, distinguishing them from other creatures. When humans employ rationality, they have access to truths about ethics under the category of natural law. Metaphysically, being may be established as something that is, and cannot be said at the same time to be something that is not. This is irrefutable, as being and nonbeing are contradictory. Ethically—or, in Aquinas's words, regarding "practical reason"—we may assert as a first principle that "good is that which all things seek after." From this, Aquinas insists, "Good is to be done and pursued, and evil is to be

25. It is crucial to note here a common confusion of *natural law* and *natural theology*. The latter proposes that God can be known in nature. While this is partially true, as Romans 1 makes clear, what may be known is only enough for humanity to be judged for their rebellion. Divine grace bringing special revelation is required for humanity to know God redemptively. Natural law proposes generic access to morality that is unable to reach an ultimate end (i.e., salvation). See *Canons of Dort*, third and fourth main points, art. 4. See also Stephen J. Grabill, *Rediscovering the Natural Law in Reformed Theological Ethics* (Eerdmans, 2006), 1–53.

26. VanDrunen, *Natural Law*, 1.

27. Consider, for example, Richard Hooker, *The Laws of Ecclesiastical Polity in Modern English*, eds. Bradford Littlejohn et al. (Davenant Press, 2019), 1.1–16, which follows much of Aquinas's Treatise on Law.

avoided."[28] From this principle, he recognizes the basis for the inclination to survival, procreation, the rational pursuit of truth, and societal participation. Furthermore, virtue may be included in natural law inasmuch as it is fitting for a thing to be virtuous in accordance with the nature of the thing (e.g., fire to heat).[29] Thus it may be said that a "virtuous" human lives as a human. But, as we'll consider, this natural "virtue" is only penultimate, serving the good order of society (e.g., the love of a parent for a child) and not righteousness before God.

Though knowledge of natural law is accessible to all, it is not necessarily received by all. In sin, humans choose to deny this natural order in many and various ways. However, the denial of the order does not remove the knowledge of this order from the human heart. It may be canceled from the mind in practical reasoning, but it remains written on the heart. So, while there is a natural inclination to the good—that is, an ordering unto the good—there is a rejection of the good in concupiscence. As Augustine says, we act against natural law because of "a distaste for well-doing, and a lustiness of iniquity," and sin "pleased us all the more because it was not permitted."[30]

The basis for natural law is found, first, in God's created order of the world. Humanity was tasked with purposes according to their nature as God's image bearers (Gen. 1:26–28). Through sin, a curse and disorder came upon the creation, with cosmic impact. However, this did not mean total devastation but frustration and the need for redemption. The creation would need to be freed from the curse in order to be perfected in eschatological fullness. In this frustrated estate, and in preparation for the Savior, God provided for the world a common covenant after he judged the violence and rebellion of

28. Aquinas, *Summa Theologica* I-II, q. 94, a. 2.

29. This, Richard Hooker understands, is the "mother of all the edicts, statutes, and decrees in the Law of Nature": "We know things either as they are in themselves or as they are in relation to one another. Knowledge of both what man is in himself and what he is in relation to all other things." Hooker, *Laws of Ecclesiastical Polity*, 1.8.6:74.

30. Augustine, *The Confessions* 2.4.9 (*NPNF*[1] 1:57).

the world in the deluge. In Genesis 8:21–9:17, God made a covenant that extended to the entire cosmos, serving as a common and universal declaration of provision (8:21–22; 9:9–10). Within this promise, the Lord also specified a particular order once more for the creation, now in a postlapsarian state: the divine image was reaffirmed in humanity as a mark of distinction and dignity. This declaration of the preservation and endurance of the divine image framed a basic system of justice specified for civil life on earth. Furthermore, God gave humanity renewed tasks to perform on the earth, modified for life after the fall (9:1–7).

VanDrunen highlights the significance of the Noahic covenant as a foundation of natural law.[31] This covenant ensures natural law's divine origins, not simply human moral autonomy; it accounts for life after the fall, and it is universal and nonredemptive.[32] Enshrined among these reasons is a response to the accusation of the naturalistic fallacy that is often directed to natural law following David Hume. VanDrunen notes that natural law existed from the beginning, and therefore notions of purpose precede the fall and any corruption of being, knowledge, or purpose. The naturalistic fallacy only stands if humanity is conceived of as nonmoral. On the contrary, natural law posits that "moral obligation is *inherent* to human nature,"[33] and this by divine design. VanDrunen concludes, "Moral obligation, therefore, was not something that human beings could know only from the outside, by positive divine command. Moral obligation was something that human beings could know by knowing themselves, in relation to the world around them."[34]

The content of the natural law is not codified in discrete rules but rather should be conceived of as a normative moral order.[35] God

31. VanDrunen, *Divine Covenants*, 95–132; *Politics After Christendom*, 56–123.
32. VanDrunen, *Divine Covenants*, 100.
33. VanDrunen, *Divine Covenants*, 87.
34. VanDrunen, *Divine Covenants*, 87.
35. VanDrunen, *Divine Covenants*, 15.

reveals this order through divine revelation in what is classically called general revelation. That it is revealed as such does not make it any less divine in its source. Hooker says it well: "Since God is Nature's author, her voice is merely His instrument."[36] As I've stressed from the beginning of this chapter, natural law accords with God's eternal law and the divine law. So, while not a complete ethical system, natural law serves as a guide for moral deliberation and serves wisdom.[37] As we'll now turn to see, human beings depend upon natural law for guidance in the formulation of legislation to govern societies.

Deciding Law for Civil Order: Human Law

As part of God's providence for the world, he has ordained that civil authorities should rule according to human law (Rom. 13:1–7). Human law is the just rules for society decided by human authorities with an interest in the common good. As the rule of natural law is challenged in humans due to concupiscence, human law is a gift from God to curtail the effects of sin in society, "restraining evil by force and fear."[38] Human law is not in direct relation to the eternal law or even the natural law but is truly related to these in so much as it accords with justice. I have considered this topic under the broader heading of the civil kingdom because human law operates in the realm of God's common grace. The distinction between natural law and human law is that natural law is directly given by God, whereas human law is an institution given by God in which the laws themselves are decided by rulers. The source material for these laws, when human law is functioning best, is natural law, from which authorities will reason practically about the common good of the society over which they govern.

36. Hooker, *Laws of Ecclesiastical Polity*, 1.8.3.
37. VanDrunen, *Divine Covenants*, 15.
38. Aquinas, *Summa Theologica* I-II, q. 95, a. 1.

Since human law is only indirectly related to God as its source, can we say that human law is binding on the moral conscience? The first inclination of believers should be to submit to authority, as civil authorities, in some ways, represent God as the ultimate authority (Rom. 13:4, 6). Again, they are agents of good (temporal) in the world, allowing for penultimate justice and peace to be pursued in a society. So long as a ruler and human laws are committed to justice, there should be submission. However, there are limits to worldly authority. First, not all earthly authority *is* just. There are those who misuse power and their position for personal gain rather than the common good. Second, there are some instances when the human law would contravene divine law. In this way, it is most certainly unjust. In such cases, "we must obey God rather than men" (Acts 5:29).[39] However, Aquinas adds a word of caution at this point: Where the observance of the law does not lead to any immediate risk, a diplomatic solution should be pursued; only in the instance of immediate risk should a law not be kept and judged against by an individual.[40] Without such a restriction, there is a risk of each individual functioning as an authority *over* the law, undermining the very foundations of society.

Before turning to consider the divine law for the redemptive kingdom, I offer some concluding remarks on the significance of the civil kingdom and God's common grace. Bonhoeffer stresses that one of the best things Christians can do is respect the penultimate and enforce it.[41] This is not because the penultimate will last but because the penultimate is necessary for the coming of the ultimate. Christians must never mistake the penultimate for the ultimate but instead allow the ultimate to shine forth through us in the midst of

39. Aquinas, *Summa Theologica* I-II, q. 96, a. 4.

40. Aquinas, *Summa Theologica* I-II, q. 96, a. 6.

41. Dietrich Bonhoeffer, *Ethics*, vol. 6 of DBW, ed. Clifford J. Green, trans. Reinhard Krauss et al (Fortress, 2005), 165–66.

the penultimate. It is only because the Son of God took on flesh that the penultimate shows forth its significance and is redirected to the ultimate.[42] Allowing the ultimate to swallow up the penultimate now would mean we are attempting to bring the future into the present. For now, the penultimate persists as the domain of calling sinners to the Savior, for them to be delivered "from the domain of darkness and transferred to the kingdom of his beloved Son" (Col. 1:13). God's providential sustaining of a world order by common grace, even after the rejection of ultimate order, is a mercy that allows his redeeming grace to go forth.

Redemption: Particular Grace for the Redemptive Kingdom

The redemptive kingdom is the domain that encompasses the elect people of God in the world. For this kingdom, God provides particular saving grace to those he has chosen from before the foundation of the world (Eph. 1:3–6). This kingdom is, in this age, the foretaste of the kingdom of God that will be known in its fullness (consummation) at the return of Christ. Though a spiritual domain, spatially and socially God's kingdom exists as the church, with ecclesial authority resting in the Word of God.[43] In accordance with his particular grace, God reveals moral knowledge of divine law through special revelation. This guides believers toward their proper end and regulates their worship and relationship to God.

Knowing Through Special Revelation: Divine Law

The divine law is to be distinguished from the natural law in the mode of delivery and ends. Since the fall of humanity, natural law

42. Bonhoeffer, *Ethics*, 174.

43. Contrast this with the state's authority. State authorities rule with the sword of civil justice (Rom. 13:3–4), while ecclesial authorities rule with the "sword of the Spirit, which is the Word of God" (Eph. 6:17).

could not perfect humanity. The divine law was offered as a mode of restoring right relationship with God. We can consider this divine law in two parts: the old and the new. The old law is that which was delivered to the people of Israel, especially through the prophet Moses. This law was unable to perfect humans in righteousness because sinful humans could not fulfill the law's demands. In this way, the old law served as a tutor, instructing the people of Israel about the righteous demands of a holy God, exposing their need, and anticipating a Savior.

The new law is that which comes through Christ in his gospel. The law of Christ offers righteousness to all who receive Christ by faith, as he has fulfilled all the divine law's demands. This law is followed by faith through the gracious empowering of the Holy Spirit, communicating righteousness to his followers through imputation. The new law, therefore, is the fulfillment of the old law, advancing those who are under the new law further in moral awareness, ability, and status.[44] "For God has done what the law, weakened by the flesh, could not do. By sending his own Son in the likeness of sinful flesh and for sin, he condemned sin in the flesh, in order that the righteous requirement of the law might be fulfilled in us, who walk not according to the flesh but according to the Spirit" (Rom. 8:3–4).

The divine law is not in opposition to the natural law, but instead finds great agreement with the natural law, and the eternal law before it. Francis Turretin notes the relationship between the natural law and the divine—or as he calls it, "moral"—law, seeing great agreement in

44. I have not here explored the differences between the law in the OT and the experience of the law in the life of NT believers. This is a perennial theological and ethical question. At the risk of being too simplistic, I offer the following summary: I accept the classic Reformed position that there is both continuity and discontinuity between the two. Following the Thirty-Nine Articles (Art. 7), I believe the old law can be divided into three: moral, civil, and ceremonial. The civil and ceremonial laws of Israel are not required of Christians, but the moral law abides. This is expounded and advanced in the NT, in what is called the law of Christ (Gal. 6:2). This law is summarized in Gal. 5:6, "For in Christ Jesus neither circumcision nor uncircumcision counts for anything, but only faith working through love."

substance and principle but distinction in "accidents and with regard to conclusions."[45] Along with this, there is a distinction in the mode of delivery, as I've already noted, between general and special revelation. The necessity of these different modes is the result of the fall.

Turretin gives five reasons why such a divine law was necessary.[46] First, it was necessary to confirm natural law, which has been doubted and muddled because of sin. As noted above, natural law is not something codified in a set of fixed rules but instead is an order of existence known rationally through perception and conscience. Divine law makes specific those things assumed under natural law, explaining how and why things are ordered as they are. Second, divine law sets about correcting those things that went awry and were corrupted by the fall. Third, natural law needed to be supplemented in the things left wanting that had been "obliterated." Fourth, the divine law was needed so that the necessity of a mediator might be known, and the desire for such mediation might be "enkindled more strongly on account of the weakness of man and of the law in the flesh." And fifth, it was needed to join Israel together as a nation and set them apart from the other nations. This, in the initial instance of the old law, was a measure of preparation for understanding the holiness and uniqueness of YHWH and the righteous requirements of those who would be called his people (Lev. 11:44). As God calls a people together in Christ from every tribe, tongue, and nation, the same characteristic of holiness applies (1 Pet. 1:15–16).

One of the crucial differences between the old and new presentations of divine law is that access to knowledge of and participation in the law of Christ is Spirit-empowered. The old law was pursued in the weakness of the flesh and thereby unable to justify. The new law offers

45. Francis Turretin, *Institutes of Elenctic Theology*, 3 vols., trans. George Musgrave Giger, ed. James T. Dennison Jr. (P&R, 1994), 2:11.1.12.

46. Turretin, *Institutes*, 2:11.1.13. What follows is a summary of Turretin's points with my own exposition of his argument.

justification by faith in Christ and enjoins believers to Christ in the power of the Spirit. Therefore, there is a *newness* of life under a new law. Believers are empowered to perform good works. What is most remarkable is that these works are unto ultimate ends. Believers do truly righteous deeds, not because they are suited to such ultimate achievement on their own but because they are equipped by the grace of God. In this way, there is no boasting but only praise to God, who is the Life-Giver.

Conclusion

The study of law and the governance of the world's two kingdoms brings into sharp focus the theological foundation of morality. Throughout this book I have been contending for a real moral order that is grounded in the goodness of God and his acts in history. In this chapter, we have seen the coherence of this order even across two kingdoms and through various modes of knowing. We conclude, therefore, that there is a universal moral order that warrants universal accountability.

As I began this chapter, I noted the tension of what is known and to what people are held to account. The resolution to this tension, at least in part, is located in the gracious provision of God. Human beings are graciously allowed to live life despite their rebellion against God. This rebellion may be unconscious, but there is enough in the order of the world (natural law) to hold all human beings to account before God (Rom. 1:18–25). The challenge, then, is not lack of information, but perception. There is enough known by all for there to be genuine accountability before God. This is, perhaps, an important correction to many common perceptions of judgment today, locating judgment in the rejection of Christ. People are not judged because of their rejection of special revelation, though this may increase judgment in some instances. People are rejected for their sinful rebellion against God their Creator. Special revelation is significant, therefore, not as the basis of judgment but as the basis of redemption.

Perception, then, is very important when considering morality and domains of life. God's special revelation is good for *all* of life, even confirming the natural law. It is God's particular provision for the elect to discover their ultimate moral order. But natural law is good for all civil life, serving as the basis of common morality, and the means provided for penultimate goods. Christians can recognize the coherence between eternal law, natural law, and divine law. But Christians will be wise to adjudicate which source is best for appeals in each domain. In public, when appealing for change to human laws, it will be best to appeal to natural law, recognizing its congruence with divine law. In public, the gospel is but "folly" (1 Cor. 1:18–31). But in the church, the divine law rules, as wisdom is imparted, not that "taught by human wisdom but taught by the Spirit, interpreting spiritual truths to those who are spiritual" (2:13).

Universal accountability is often looked upon as a problem to be solved, but this should not be so. It is part of the good news of the gospel. In Revelation, an angel has an "eternal gospel to proclaim to those who dwell on the earth, to every nation and tribe and language and people." This gospel is, "Fear God and give him glory, because the hour of his judgment has come, and worship him who made heaven and earth, the sea and the springs of water" (Rev. 14:6–7). The eternal gospel promises universal judgment before God. Emil Brunner explains, "Whatever God demands can only be universal, that is, valid for all men, even if those who do not hear this demand do not admit this validity, and indeed do not understand the claim to universal validity. The believer alone clearly perceives that the Good, as it is recognized in faith, is the sole Good, and that all that is otherwise called good cannot lay claim to this title, at least not in the ultimate sense of the word."[47]

47. Emil Brunner, *The Divine Imperative: A Study in Christian Ethics*, trans. Olive Wyon (Lutterworth Press, 1964), 89–90.

The universal validity, as Brunner notes, is something that *is*, even if not recognized. This is *good news*—gospel. It is good because it means there is an order in this world, and because there is an order, there will be justice. Those who commit atrocities now—from the seemingly small acts of individual selfish indulgence to grand-scale violence and genocide—will be held to account. There is a moral order, and it matters. The guarantee of this order is God himself.

Having explored how moral knowledge comes to humans and what they are accountable for, we move in the next chapter to examine how Scripture presents the moral order. Rather than seeing morality in the Bible as limited to a single mode of reasoning, we will see multiple modes delivered for a single moral vision that God's goodness unites.

7

A Diverse but Unified Moral Vision

Biblical Modes of Ethical Reasoning

In a word, the action to which love impels is the action which is characterized as the fulfilment of the law. Again, since love is in the category of feeling which creates affinity with the object and constrains the outflow of affection for the object, the fulfilment which love constrains is not the fulfilment coerced and unwilling formal compliance, but the fulfilment of cheerful and willing obedience. Without such constraining and impelling love there is really no fulfilment of the law.[1]

John Murray

THE MAIN PROBLEM RELATED TO contemporary ethics is what mode of reasoning should dominate or govern our morality.

1. John Murray, *Principles of Conduct: Aspects of Biblical Ethics* (Eerdmans, 1957), 22.

This problem is created by the pursuit of ethics without direct access to, or belief in, the metaphysical foundations of the moral order. Immanuel Kant, for instance, working on a rational ethical system, postulates a categorical imperative—one law to rule all. Obedience to principle matters most, irrespective of the outcome. Others, such as Jeremy Bentham, take an opposing position, looking to humanity and our collective desires to present pleasure and pain as ruling principles undergirding a utilitarian ethical system. In such a system, the outcome is paramount. Whatever charitable judgment we may wish to pass on these endeavors, they are failures. Their foundations are *within* the cosmos, most explicitly in humanity.[2] Furthermore, they set certain goods against others because there is no way to account for unity among different ethical modes. In short, they fail to capture the God-given order of things.

In this chapter, I will explore the various modes of ethical reasoning in Scripture to discover a united moral vision grounded in the unity of God himself. We will see, once more, that the moral order is objective, received through revelation. Christians do well to apprentice themselves to Scripture, discovering how the Bible presents the moral vision for the world in different ways and across various circumstances. The goal of this investigation is instruction on how Scripture can serve our contemporary moral deliberation.

2. To be fair, these systems did not necessarily negate the notion of God; in fact, Kant assumed God as the basis for order, being the supreme cause. However, the moral order was to be understood, or rather moral obligation recognized, through rationality. He believed God was only our basis of moral goodness because of the *idea* we could cognize. Kant desired a moral philosophy that preserved the autonomy of the individual will. He believed rational order is something humans press on the world, and only where there is an unconditional law—the categorical imperative—could there be true freedom. Simply put, Kant pursued a pure form of morals without consideration of any circumstance, experience, or outcome. The purity of his "metaphysics of morals" would be found in "pure philosophy." See Immanuel Kant, *Groundwork of the Metaphysics of Morals*, trans. and ed. Mary Gregor (Cambridge University Press, 1997).

The Grounds of a Unified Moral Vision: God and His Word

In the last chapter, I examined Thomas Aquinas's fourfold approach to law, carried forward by many after him. The unity of eternal, natural, and divine law is clearly grounded in God himself. This frames all that is. Therefore, there is coherence to the order of things because God is the sovereign ruler over all. We saw that this sovereignty over the world and the provision of a moral order extends to both common and redeemed life. As we look more closely at divine law, we examine what is theologically called "special revelation." The means of special revelation is God speaking his word through the prophets, and ultimately sending his Word, the eternal Son, Jesus Christ.

Though Holy Scripture comprises material from a period extending more than a millennium, written by nearly forty authors, Christians believe all of it is *God's* word. The Scriptures are *theopneustos*—God-breathed—which grounds their efficacy for "teaching, for reproof, for correction, and for training in righteousness," leading to the people of God being "complete, equipped for every good work" (2 Tim. 3:16–17). The significance of the divine origin of Scripture for ethics cannot be overstated. There is an intimate link between right doctrine and moral practice.

In his First Epistle to Timothy, the apostle Paul expresses concern about heterodoxy, the teaching of "different doctrine" (1 Tim. 1:3). The root of Paul's concern is that the church in Ephesus would be established in "sound doctrine" that accords with "the gospel of the glory of the blessed God" (1:10–11). The consequence of following poor doctrine is all sorts of immoral behavior (1:9–10; cf. 6:3–5). Paul includes a personal example detailing the kinds of sin that he lived in—blaspheming, persecuting believers, opposing the gospel—saying he had acted ignorantly in "unbelief" (1:14) before he received God's mercy (1:16). Paul's desire for Timothy and the Ephesians is a life that accords with the faith.

Good doctrine and moral living go hand in hand. One can have good doctrine and refuse to live by it (e.g., Hymenaeus and Alexander in 1 Tim. 1:19–20), but one will not live properly without good doctrine. This conviction is the baseline of Paul's exhortation to pray that the nations would be saved and "come to the knowledge of the truth" (2:4). Timothy, having been trained in the "words of faith and the good doctrine," was also to train himself in godliness (4:6–7). Paul encourages Timothy to "keep a close watch on yourself and on the teaching" (4:15), for in doing so he would save himself and his hearers (4:16). Bad belief lies at the foundation of moral misconduct. But good belief also requires positive action. Sound doctrine is necessary for healthy morality, but belief *alone* is not enough. Indeed, one may claim right beliefs and be deeply unrighteous. Faith must work (cf. James 2:17, 26).

Righteousness—the biblical word that most clearly and succinctly captures a moral life—is simple for God but not for humans. God's being *is* simple, and his acts accord with his being. God's simplicity accords with his perfection. But human beings are not simple, nor are they perfect. Our righteousness involves a recognition of purpose and a conscientious orientation to that purpose. Furthermore, our morality is not simply right *acts*, nor is it simply right *character*. Righteousness is aligning both internal and external life to a proper end. This is apparent in the Old Testament prophets' warnings about religious practices that were seemingly conducted in "right" ways but with corrupt hearts. So, the Lord spoke through the prophet Isaiah, "Bring no more vain offerings; incense is an abomination to me. New moon and Sabbath and the calling of convocations—I cannot endure iniquity and solemn assembly" (Isa. 1:13). Jesus picks up this theme from Isaiah when responding to the Pharisees: "This people honors me with their lips, but their heart is far from me; in vain do they worship me, teaching as doctrines the commandments of men" (Mark 7:6–7; cf. Isa. 29:13). Not only must the heart align with true practice, but true practice is also determined by God, our ultimate end.[3]

Of course, the alignment of human beings in heart and action unto our ultimate end is fraught with difficulty. We've seen, in an earlier chapter, the implications of original sin for humanity's ongoing moral life. If right actions will proceed from the heart, the heart needs renewal. Regeneration is the only hope for humans to live righteously. The promise of the new covenant is precisely this renewal: "And I will give you a new heart, and a new spirit I will put within you. And I will remove the heart of stone from your flesh and give you a heart of flesh. And I will put my Spirit within you, and cause you to walk in my statutes and be careful to obey my rules" (Ezek. 36:26–27). This righteous way of being comes from the empowerment of the Holy Spirit. But this righteousness is not our own; it is our participation in the life of Christ by faith. Faith is subjective, not objective. So our faith is only as sure as the object of our faith. This means that it is not *faith* that is righteousness, but faith *in* Jesus Christ, the righteous One. In him, we "become the righteousness of God" (2 Cor. 5:21). Thus, the apostle Paul says, "through the Spirit, by faith, we ourselves eagerly wait for the hope of righteousness" (Gal. 5:5). The hope of moral righteousness is never in our subjective person, but in our participation in Christ.

But faith is not morally stagnant. Faith will rest in the righteousness of Christ and live accordingly. New life will manifest itself in good works. The apostle Paul makes this connection plain in several of his epistles. He reminds the Ephesians that by grace they have been saved through faith (Eph. 2:8). They are created in Christ

3. In Paul's exhortation to Timothy, the "end" for which "we toil and strive" is godliness. This is a summary of life lived obediently to true doctrine. This is not self-determined (or demonically determined, 1 Tim. 4:1–2) but instead divinely ordained, as is evident in Paul's contrast of this way with that of the ascetics (1 Tim. 4). Godliness is what Timothy was to be "trained" in, following his training in the "words of faith and good doctrine" (4:6–8).

Jesus for good works (2:10). Similarly, he reminds Titus that salvation is owing to the lovingkindness, goodness, and mercy of God, not to human works (Titus 3:4–5). But having been washed and renewed by the Holy Spirit (3:5), those who have believed in God now must devote themselves to good works (3:8). Redemption was for purification before God and zeal for good works (2:14). In each of these instances, Paul demonstrates that the renewal that comes through redemption is intended for good works. Changed hearts are expressed in a changed way of living with a clear view toward an ultimate end. God acts to bring righteousness and commands our righteous living on this basis.

Biblical Modes of Ethical Reasoning

Multiple ethical modes in Scripture direct the righteous life. I mentioned earlier that some modern systems see certain ethical modes as opposed, such as deontological and consequentialist ethics. This is, of course, true. A rule and an outcome will be in tension, such as the famous tension of Dietrich Bonhoeffer being involved in an assassination plot. Would the outcome of potentially ending war and genocide justify breaking the rule "do not murder"? Biblically, this tension was present in Abraham's call to sacrifice the son of promise (Gen. 22). If Abraham acted only for an outcome—namely, preserving the promised heir—he would need to disregard the command of God to offer a sacrifice. This, in the end, proved a test of faith for Abraham. Other commands seem to be more self-serving. The Pharisees classically paraded acts of righteousness in public but lacked the heart to make their deeds truly righteous. How do we account for seemingly different modes of ethical reasoning, sometimes felt in tension? In this section, I will demonstrate briefly how different modes are featured in Scripture and work together in a unified theological vision of morality.

Law/Command

Law locates goodness with an act, rather than the actor or outcome. Law may be the primary mode most would identify with biblical morality.[4] The Ten Commandments (or Decalogue), of course, are exemplary in the dominance of this mode. Likewise, in Jesus's most famous discourse—the Sermon on the Mount—he offers an exposition of some of the broader commands in the Torah, framing them and advancing them in view of his kingdom. Commandments serve to order moral expectations, determining boundaries and requirements of moral action. As boundaries, they negatively frame what should not be done. As requirements, they express positive initiatives that must be taken. Classically, the two tables of the law serve to orient life in the community, both living before God and with neighbors.

Law remains necessary for a moral vision of the world because of human concupiscence. The will of God for humans has always been formulated in some sense as law. The initial commands for Adam—positively in the tasks associated with bearing the image of God and negatively in the prohibition of the fruit of the tree of knowledge of good and evil—were primitive introductions to God's will for humanity. After the fall, further instruction was required with regard to the divine will. Calvin understood the moral law as an extension of what was present elsewhere, but specified for debased minds. "It is a fact that the law of God which we call the moral law is nothing else than a testimony of natural law and of that conscience which God has engraved upon the minds of men."[5] The debased minds of humans require instruction in the divine will. This remains true for regenerate Christians. Even though their reason

4. I am using law in the common notion of commands here. This is distinct from the Thomistic understanding of law explored in the previous chapter. Law, here, is part of what Aquinas explores as "divine law," something that also encompasses other special revelations of morality.

5. John Calvin, *Institutes of the Christian Religion*, ed. John T. McNeill, trans. Ford Lewis Battles (Westminster, 1960), 4.20.16.

is sanctified (e.g., the renewal of the mind that leads to transformation, Rom. 12:2), the law is necessary for exposing corruption and instructing them in the upright path so that they can discern the will of God.

A perennial challenge to law as an ethical mode is the rigidity accompanying the legalistic employment of law. Legalism lacks creativity, unable to deploy the law in new contexts. It demands that every situation be accommodated to the law, rather than the law creatively applied to a context. Furthermore, legalism seeks righteousness in perfect adherence to the law irrespective of circumstance. But as we know from good judicial systems, the law must be applied, and this application is not simple. Good judgment demands interpretation of law and consideration of circumstance. So, good judgment about the moral law in the Christian life must interpret a given law delivered to a person/people in one context and consider if/how that law continues to remain effective and applicable in a new context.

For Protestants, law as an ethical mode is further complicated by the juxtaposition of law and gospel introduced by Martin Luther. In the interest of promoting justification by faith, law was put in strong contrast to gospel truth. This was built on a reading of the apostle Paul in Galatians, in particular, in which pursuing justification by law is antithetical to gospel grace: "You are severed from Christ, you who would be justified by the law; you have fallen away from grace" (5:4). The question raised by a strong law-and-gospel duality is how good works (positive moral action) fit within the Christian life. J. de Waal Dryden identifies this as an irreconcilable tension for those following Luther: "In the context of justification, faith and works are absolutely *antithetical*, but when we move to sanctification faith and works are *complementary*, and faith is necessarily expressed in works."[6] For many Protestants, protecting justification has remained

6. J. de Waal Dryden, *A Hermeneutic of Wisdom: Recovering the Formative Agency of Scripture* (Baker Academic, 2018), 65. See also Oliver O'Donovan, *Resurrection and Moral Order: An Outline for Evangelical Ethics*, 2nd ed. (Eerdmans, 1994), 151–56. Defending

the priority, and the place of works in the Christian life has remained ambiguous because of the perceived tension. This has resulted in an underdeveloped theology of the Christian life, dwelling more on conversion *from* sin and less on conversion *to* new life.

In the Reformed tradition, there is a stronger legacy of law as the basis of moral theology. Many Reformed ecclesial traditions have captured the place of the law in the Christian life through the threefold division of the law—civil, ceremonial, and moral—with the moral law continuing to apply to Christian living. The law serves Christians by alerting them to their sinfulness and offering them moral guidance. But this has also presented its own challenges. For instance, which of the laws are moral? Are the civil and ceremonial laws devoid of moral content? The simplest set of moral laws has been identified with the Decalogue,[7] but these cannot be the only moral laws. Jesus and the apostles draw on many other laws as the basis of their moral teaching in the New Testament. A basic hermeneutical principle has been to follow the lead of the New Testament's witness, both in its interpretation and application of the law.

Virtue/Character

A second scriptural mode of ethical reasoning is virtue/character, which locates goodness within the actor rather than the action or outcome. When we discern intention or motivation, we look beyond an action to the one acting. Virtues are the habits that direct the will to act well.[8] They are matters of character leading an actor to be moral in any

the Lutheran position, Brunner believes Martin Luther was the one who had taken the "ethical problem" most seriously since the apostles. Brunner sees only two human options for morality: eudaemonism or legalism. What liberates the Christian from these two options is faith. Emil Brunner, *The Divine Imperative: A Study in Christian Ethics*, trans. Olive Wyon (Lutterworth Press, 1964), 57–58.

7. E.g., Westminster Confession of Faith 19.2.

8. Petrus van Mastricht, *Faith in the Triune God*, vol. 2. of *Theoretical-Practical Theology*, ed. Joel R. Beeke, trans. Todd M. Rester (Reformation Heritage, 2019), 305–6.

situation. Jonathan Edwards says, "Virtue is the beauty of the qualities and exercises of the heart, or those actions which proceed from them."[9] Edwards appreciates the moral nature of these qualities. He recognizes a close relationship between actions and the internal characteristics impacting the will and disposition, commonly called the "heart."

Virtue recognizes that morality is never to be reduced simply to an act, for good acts can be done with bad intentions. For example, a kiss may be given as a sign of love, but it is not truly a loving act unless there is a genuine disposition of love (Mark 14:44–46). Likewise, though the Israelites offered sacrifices, these were often practiced without the appropriate conviction. Their service to God was simply lip service (Isa. 29:13–14). Such acts of worship, while honorable with a true heart, are detestable acts of hypocrisy with a false heart. Jesus says, "For no good tree bears bad fruit, nor again does a bad tree bear good fruit, for each tree is known by its own fruit. For figs are not gathered from thornbushes, nor are grapes picked from a bramble bush. The good person out of the good treasure of his heart produces good, and the evil person out of his evil treasure produces evil, for out of the abundance of the heart his mouth speaks" (Luke 6:43–45). Deeds will only be as good as the heart behind them.

The connection between the heart and deeds raises two interesting moral dilemmas. First, can someone without a regenerated heart be virtuous? I have already demonstrated the need for spiritual renewal for truly righteous living. Do Christians, then, have an exclusive claim to virtue? In short, no. Virtue as a moral mode predates Christ and has been discussed in many other religious and philosophical traditions. The most noteworthy historical example is Aristotle's *Nicomachean Ethics*. This work serves as the foundation for many other explorations of virtue theory, including that of Augustine, Aquinas,

9. Jonathan Edwards, "A Dissertation Concerning the Nature of True Virtue," in vol. 1 of *The Works of Jonathan Edwards*, ed. Edward Hickman (Banner of Truth, 1974), 122.

and Edwards. But though virtue theory was present in Aristotle, the distinctive claim of Christianity is that true virtue is only present in those who are regenerate. Edwards argues that "love to God is most essential to true virtue; and that no benevolence whatsoever to other beings can be of the nature of true virtue without it."[10] This claim is grounded in the Aristotelean notion that true virtue will be directed toward a chief end. For Edwards, without clear theological orientation, all attempts at virtue would ultimately fail.

Second, connecting the heart and deeds raises the dilemma of whether the intention is all that matters. If a bad deed is done with good intentions, does that make the deed acceptable morally? Or, if a good deed is done with bad intentions, is the deed bad? Augustine grapples with this tension when he considers what distinguished the *traditio*—"giving over"—of Jesus by Judas and the Father. For Augustine, the differentiator was intention: "The diverse intention therefore makes the things done diverse. Though the thing be one, yet if we measure it by the diverse intentions, we find the one a thing to be loved, the other to be condemned; the one we find a thing to be glorified, the other to be detested. Such is the force of charity. See that it alone discriminates, it alone distinguishes the doings of men."[11] In the act, it was the virtue (or vice) that accompanied the act that served to distinguish the same event.[12] This does not mean that all acts are permissible with charity, but instead that the same act can be judged differently when intention is considered.[13]

10. Edwards, "True Virtue," 1:126.

11. Augustine, *Ten Homilies on the First Epistle of John* (*NPNF*[1] 7:504).

12. There are potential problems with Augustine's reasoning here if this episode is taken in isolation. In other words, charity cannot justify any act. If so, many heinous acts would be permissible because of intention. Elsewhere, Augustine employs deontological reasoning to express the wrongness of some acts. See Augustine, *To Consentius: Against Lying* (*Contra Mendacium*) and *On Lying* (*De Mendacio*) in vol. 3 of *NPNF*[1].

13. It is important to note that God is *sui generis* and moral judgment of God's acts must always be affirmative. Any judgment otherwise is idolatrous.

Having considered these two dilemmas, we may conclude that true virtue is required for the moral life, and only ever possible for the heart that is regenerated by the Holy Spirit. The Spirit works new life in the Christian so that what once was dead begins to produce fruit (Gal. 5:16–26). This fruit is evidence of the life now found in Christ. Positively, Christians are called to *be*, not just *act*. Character must be cultivated, even habituated (Col. 3:12–17). Furthermore, the old ways of viciousness must be mortified (Col. 3:5–11; cf. Rom. 8:13). But while there is a strong call to obedience both in act and will, it is the Spirit who works to change the desires of the heart, so that the Christian may be virtuous (Phil. 2:12–13). Augustine likens this to an emperor leading an army: Christ rules over minds by his Spirit, commanding virtues as ministers to do his will.[14]

Purpose/Consummation

The unifying element of both law and virtue is purpose (telos). God commands according to his purposes, and he desires virtue that is attuned to love him, our ultimate end. Creation begins with purpose, and this purpose is realized at the consummation of history. Once more, note the significance of Christ for our moral understanding and being. In Jesus's judgment on the cross, we see the condemnation of all that is wrong in the world, distorted from its original purpose. In Jesus's resurrection, we see the redemption of creation, rather than its abandonment. In the expectation of Jesus's return, we hope for a new creation. Not only is the original purpose of creation sustained and achieved, but it is also carried forward to its fulfillment. "All things were created through him and for him" (Col. 1:16). The sin

14. "There is as it were an army of an emperor seated within in thy mind. For as an emperor by his army does what he will, so the Lord Jesus Christ, once beginning to dwell in our inner man, (*i.e.* in the mind through faith), uses these virtues as His ministers." Augustine, *Ten Homilies* (*NPNF*[1] 7:506).

of humanity could not and would not thwart the purposes of God. He himself brings the world to its rightful end.

Morally, this matters not just for our understanding of reality, but also for our experience. Living life with purpose is necessary for any *ordered* existence. Aristotle recognizes this fact, identifying happiness (*eudaimonia*) as the highest good for humanity. This is not wrong, even if it is misguided. For Aristotle, happiness is intellectual as much as anything else. But in Christ, we know something far greater. Our happiness is in God himself. It is not happiness in an idea—something abstract and impersonal—but in a personal being. "Therefore, in so far as all men seek a happy life, they are not in error. . . . When the supreme good is sought and gained, a man is happy, and this we all undoubtedly desire."[15] Eudaemonism is wrong when happiness is self-referential or self-determined, but the pursuit of happiness itself is not wrong. We must realize, however, that true happiness is known when we desire and live toward our chief end. Edwards may put it best: "The true goodness of a thing, must be its agreeableness to its *end*, or its fitness to answer the design for which it was made. Therefore, they are good moral agents, whose temper of mind, or propensity of heart, is agreeable to the *end* for which God made moral agents."[16]

Apprentices of Scripture

The challenge of Gotthold Lessing's "ugly ditch" between history and eternal truths is well-rehearsed. For our purposes, the problem could be stated this way: How does what was written nearly two millennia ago (or more)—the accidental truths of history—bear on our present reality (and our moral reasoning)? One of the great challenges to thinking about history is how it relates and with what authority

15. Augustine, *The Problem of Free Choice (De Libero Arbitrio)*, vol. 22 of Ancient Christian Writers, trans. Dom Mark Pontifex (Longman, Greens and Co., 1955), 9.26.
16. Edwards, "True Virtue," 1:127.

it relates to our present context. When Jesus addresses his disciples in the Sermon on the Mount, using an example (even a hyperbolic one?) of giving in the synagogue, does it relate to us now? Were people really blowing trumpets to draw attention to their righteous acts? Is this a literal prohibition not to have musical accompaniment to giving? When you give, must you do so with one hand behind your back, so that you "do not let your left hand know what your right hand is doing"? Pressing deeper, how does giving in a synagogue in first-century Palestine relate to twenty-first-century Australia? Oliver O'Donovan asks a sharp question about the fusion of the modern with the ancient: "How can such a fusion be anything other than a selective absorption of the ancient by the modern in accordance with the laws of its own metabolism?"[17]

The answer to the ugly ditch is a theological vision of reality. The world we inhabit today is not so different from the world of yesteryear (ancient as it may be). In fact, from the viewpoint of the biblical canon, we are living in the same epoch of history as the apostles—between the ascension of Christ and his impending return. The world they address and the theological vision they set forth is for the time we still inhabit. This means that though the canon is "closed," its vision for history is still current. God transcends time with a word that is living and active, not static (Heb. 4:12), and this word exposes all and holds them to account (v. 13).

Furthermore, history reassures us of genuine meaning and understanding. We comprehend new situations in view of a history of happenings before us. In this way, while there are "new" situations, they belong to a very real order in which these "new" things make sense. O'Donovan explains, "Without a generic order new things would indeed be incomprehensible, for they would be absolutely particular, which is beyond the power of human thought to grasp. The utterly

17. O'Donovan, *Resurrection and Moral Order*, 162.

'unique situation,' if we were ever to encounter it, would destroy us and the universe. . . . Thus wisdom greets new things with recognition, and new moral decisions can be made."[18]

Kevin Vanhoozer contends that there is an even more pressing challenge—a new ditch—for theologians in our day: How does theology relate to practice?[19] In other words, while historical relevance may be settled theologically, how this theological truth translates to practice presents a further chasm. This divide had been exacerbated in modern times by the separation of biblical and theological studies. Integral to retrieving a healthy link between theology and practice, Vanhoozer argues, is the theological interpretation of Scripture.[20] Scripture must be received as God's word to us about reality, not critically as if it were up to us to decide whether it is canonical or authoritative, or what bearing it does or should have on our lives. Theological interpretation will understand each discrete biblical section within a wider canonical and theological frame. In this way, the reading will inform theology, but theology will also instruct the reading.[21]

For theology to be "done" properly, it can never be for *information* alone; it must be for guidance and transformation. Theology instructs us about God and his relationship to his creation. This knowledge, rightly received, will lead to worship. *Reception* is an important concept because it delineates what may be known from what

18. O'Donovan, *Resurrection and Moral Order*, 189.

19. Kevin J. Vanhoozer, *The Drama of Doctrine: A Canonical-Linguistic Approach to Christian Theology* (Westminster John Knox, 2005), 12–13.

20. Vanhoozer, *Drama of Doctrine*, 20.

21. I've written elsewhere about this. In relation to the work of preaching, see Chase R. Kuhn, "Theology for Preaching, Preaching for Theology," in *Theology Is for Preaching: Biblical Foundations, Method, and Practice*, ed. Chase R. Kuhn and Paul Grimmond (Lexham Press, 2021), 1–17. In relation to the hermeneutical task, see Chase R. Kuhn, "Figural Reading Within Contemporary Theological Interpretation of Scripture: Problems and Parameters," in *Revelation and Reason in Christian Theology*, ed. David I. Starling and Christopher C. Green (Lexham Press, 2018), 127–44.

is truly understood.[22] "Failure to bear fruit is failure to hear."[23] The discernment of coherence between the text and our context is what is conventionally considered wisdom. For proper correspondence between the message of the text and its application today, the text must be understood in its context *first*. What required such a text to be delivered? What was the situation demanding such a teaching, correction, rebuke, narrative, poem, and so on? This will help the reader understand the intended aim of the text, first for its original audience. But then, because of a theological vision of the text and its ongoing relevance, the reader will seek to understand how that message continues to speak in a new context. This requires imagination.

Imagination in theology and ethics is not to be conceived of as a subjective free-for-all. The text does not bend to accommodate the reader. Rather, the imagination seeks to see the truth of the text applied in a new context. Truth is unchanging; application is situational. This act of imagination is part of the work of the Spirit in the life of the believer. Vanhoozer says, "The Spirit thus opens readers' minds and hearts so that the words can produce all their intended effects: effects of illocutionary understanding and effects of perlocutionary obedience. Again, the Spirit's role is not to add a new sense to the Word, but to energize and empower the sense—the speech act—that is already there."[24] The Spirit's work does not energize the text in a fashion that it *becomes* the Word, but rather leads the believer to imagine how the Word that *is* calls for obedience in new situations. In this way, the application of the Word is always new, always fresh, always current. When the prophet Isaiah states, "The word of our God will stand forever" (Isa. 40:8), it is not a statement of mere permanence

22. Vanhoozer employs the distinction between *scientia* and *sapientia*, recognizing that theology is always underserved when it is dismissive of the sapiential aspect.

23. Dryden, *Hermeneutic of Wisdom*, 37.

24. Kevin J. Vanhoozer, *Is There a Meaning in This Text? The Bible, the Reader, and the Morality of Literary Knowledge* (Zondervan, 1998), 428.

but of enduring significance. Scripture is not simply timeless, though it is this, but it is also perpetually timely. In this way, the gospel is continually good news. Though it was heralded to different people in different places and times, it remains a good word for all today. The goodness of this Word rests in the Word itself, even as it is heard and applied to unique lives.[25]

The move to apply, even imaginatively, is difficult to do responsibly. This difficulty is for reasons already mentioned. What is required for the faithful interpretation and application of the Scriptures—true understanding, reception—is apprenticeship to the Scriptures. "Good interpretation requires not just sweat but skill, and not just skill but character. Interpretation of the Scriptures is like a craft or a trade that must be learned if we are to draw the right connections, make the right intuitive leaps, and bring to bear on the task the right dispositions, affections, and virtues."[26] Ethics must be imagined, here, as part of this interpretive practice. The truth of the text must be lived in one's context. Learning how the moral vision of Scripture meets each new moment requires this sort of apprenticeship. We observe how God communicates the moral vision for his people through different genres and different modes of ethical reasoning in the Scriptures. We observe in the text, for example, how Jesus reads the Law and applies it to the lives of his disciples (Matt. 5–7). While we are not in the same context as his disciples, we notice *how* he applies the Scriptures. So apprenticeship is more than just knowing *what* is taught or *why* it was taught—both crucial components of understanding and application—but also *how* the message is taught in various contexts.

25. "In sum, the Word of God for today (significance) is a function of the Word of God in the text (meaning), which in turn is a witness to the living and eternal Word of God in the Trinity (referent)." Vanhoozer, *Is There a Meaning in this Text?*, 423, italics in original.

26. David I. Starling, *Hermeneutics as Apprenticeship: How the Bible Shapes Our Interpretive Habits and Practices* (Baker Academic, 2016), 17.

The challenge of moral deliberation in one's context involves multiple steps. O'Donovan proposes an algebraic formula for this process.[27] He proposes that in Scripture we may observe different trains of moral reasoning that can be presented as [A → B], where [A] represents a principle of action leading to some resolution [B]. Each of these moral trains of thought is provoked by a situation. This train of reasoning is *closed*, but it can assist us in our own reasoning about situations that remain *open* before us. Thus, in our time we will reason from [X] to [Y], where [Y] is yet to be determined. To borrow the previously mentioned metaphor of apprenticeship, those trained by the Scriptures will, in wisdom, recall a train or multiple trains of moral thought that will bear upon their own reasoning in a context. So, the [X] today will draw on one or more [A → B] reasonings in Scripture that is apt for the current moral decision. This will lead to a resolution, a decision to act. Maturing in wisdom as an apprentice is growth in discernment about what, why, and how different information is relevant to the deliberation process.

As complex as the algebraic formula may seem on the surface, it becomes very practicable when framed in less abstract terms. The [A] may be understood as *what* is taught with a specific reason *why*, the intended aim [B]. As we read each train of moral thought, we can observe *how* the biblical author communicates, paying close attention to the genre and ethical mode(s). Understanding *how* impacts what sort of ethical mode may impinge upon our situation. For instance, is there a prohibitive command? Is there an exhortation to virtue? Does the author give an example for imitation? And so on. Understanding each component in the biblical text(s) will provide a pathway for corresponding application in the new situation.

27. Oliver O'Donovan, *Self, World, and Time*, vol. 1 of *Ethics as Theology* (Eerdmans, 2013), 79–80.

But as important as anything else in this process is learning to see correlation between situations. The situation a biblical text addresses is not specifically our situation. Therefore, we must discern a process of translating a message given in one context to another. This, I believe, comes down to what I call *tension*. What in the original context demanded the train of moral thought? What question needed to be answered? What problem needed to be solved? What moral issue was contrary to the will of God? Discerning this tension in the text closely relates to understanding what is being taught and why. In other words, to discern the tension, look to the principle (*what*) and intended aim (*why*) in the moral train of thought. Understanding the tension provides the crucial link between contexts and situations, and I believe it is the key to faithfully imagining fresh moral application.

To illustrate these different components concretely, consider the earlier reference to Matthew 6:2–4, where Jesus instructs the disciples about giving.[28]

> Thus, when you give to the needy, sound no trumpet before you, as the hypocrites do in the synagogues and in the streets, that they may be praised by others. Truly, I say to you, they have received their reward. But when you give to the needy, do not let your left hand know what your right hand is doing, so that your giving may be in secret. And your Father who sees in secret will reward you.

What [A] Jesus teaches is not actually a principle in the first instance about giving, but rather the audience before whom one practices righteous deeds. Jesus teaches a searching truth about God: The Father knows the secret things. *Why* [B] Jesus teaches this is to challenge

28. I have written about this extensively in relation to the preaching task: Chase R. Kuhn, "In Defence of the 'Big Idea': Key Questions for Faithful Preaching," in *Preacher, Pastor and Evangelist: Essays on the Work of Ministry, in Honour of Simon Manchester*, ed. Gerard O'Brien (Matthias Media, 2019).

his disciples to practice their righteous deeds before the appropriate audience: God alone. *How* Jesus instructs the disciples is through an outrageous example. He helps his audience feel the inappropriateness of righteous deeds performed before a human audience, exposing human pride and folly implicitly. The *tension* in the context, then, is whether his hearers know God as their Father. If they know God as Father, then they know he knows the secret things and will live accordingly. The real cutting feature of the text is that if God knows things like deeds done in secret, then he also knows even more secret things, like the heart.

Thus, this illustration serves as one of three in Matthew 6:1–18 that support the main point Jesus is making in his moral train of thought: "Beware of practicing your righteousness before other people in order to be seen by them, for then you will have no reward from your Father who is in heaven" (v. 1). The abiding significance of this passage today is not found in relating our giving practices to those of the synagogues of Jesus's time but in connecting through the tension: Do you know the Father? If so, you will take care to perform your righteous deeds—including giving—for the appropriate audience. The imagination for a contemporary context will be drawn to consider how/where/when righteousness may be practiced for the wrong audience.

Conclusion

Theological truth must be apprehended in a way that is genuinely articulated in the Christian life. This articulation should not be done only once but is to be consistently applied imaginatively with each new moral decision and opportunity. Therefore, the Christian disciple's life is one of apprenticeship to the Scriptures, seeking to learn from them the will of God as it is presented in beautiful pluriformity. "It is possible to view canonical diversity not as a problem to be solved but as a blessing to be received with thanks. It is precisely this diversity—call it plenitude, an embarrassment of riches, a Pentecostal plurality—that enables Scripture to speak on so many levels to so many different kinds of situations."[29] As apprentices, Christians are tasked with reflecting on a theological vision of the moral order. As wisdom matures, so too does the conscience, aiding us in ready moral decision-making.[30] This, of course, is not a solo project. We are formed under the tutelage of the Scriptures, led by the Spirit, in the fellowship of God's people. It is to this community that we now turn.

29. Vanhoozer, *Drama of Doctrine*, 275.

30. "Conscience is not a foundational moral notion or an axiom from which we can proceed to positive moral doctrine, but a derivative notion whose force depends upon the functions which it is called to perform in a particular vision for the moral life." John Webster, "God and Conscience," in *Word and Church: Essays in Christian Dogmatics* (T&T Clark, 2001), 233.

8

The Church as School of Morality

> Love of God is affirmed in and through our other loves, structuring them and ordering them, so that with each new discovery of good that the world and time lay open to us, the question of the love of God is put again, its sovereignty over other loves reasserted or forgotten. For love of the world and of the God who gives the world occupies our experience not as a settled condition, but as a series of openings and adventures.[1]
>
> Oliver O'Donovan

"You do you." Recently, a friend of mine aimed to encourage me with this phrase, picked up from the common vernacular. Novelist Colson Whitehead says of such phrases: "Like black holes, they are inviolable. All criticism is destroyed when it hits the horizon of their circular logic, and not even light can escape their immense gravity. In a world where the selfie has become our dominant art form,

1. Oliver O'Donovan, *Self, World, and Time*, vol. 1 of *Ethics as Theology* (Eerdmans, 2013), 119.

tautological phrases like 'You do you' and its tribe provide a philosophical scaffolding for our ever-evolving, ever more complicated narcissism."[2] Narcissism may well be to blame, but I am not sure the cause is always as dramatic as a personality disorder. Culturally, we've been hunting for some sure footing for morality. When we gave up believing in God or a higher power ordering our world, we had to find a different foundation. This quest has failed miserably. Having nowhere stable to turn, we've turned inward to ourselves—the most "stable" place we can find.

We have highly individualized senses of morality, yet we desperately want something to agree on as a society. So, we've turned individual expression into a virtue. We're told that "one ought not to challenge another's values. That is their concern, their life choice, and it ought to be respected."[3] Morality has been relativized. We're all authorities unto ourselves, and no one is allowed to challenge us. If they do, we simply call them "haters" and do what we've decided to do. No one can tell us we're wrong.

In this chapter, we will explore one of God's purposes for the church: the moral formation of his people. As the people of God gather with other believers in Christ, they are changed into the likeness of Christ *together*. The church provides the space for morality to be tested and for transformation to be graciously and patiently cultivated. At the church's core is knowing and showing forth the love of God, according to the newness of life in the Spirit. As Christians live together in fellowship, they are together being prepared as a beautiful bride in anticipation of the return of Christ, the bridegroom. We'll begin by looking once more at the problems that combat the

2. Colson Whitehead, "How 'You Do You' Perfectly Captures Our Narcissistic Culture," *New York Times*, March 31, 2015, https://www.nytimes.com/2015/04/05/magazine/how-you-do-you-perfectly-captures-our-narcissistic-culture.html.

3. Charles Taylor, *The Ethics of Authenticity* (Harvard University Press, 1991), 13–14. Taylor is not advocating this position but taking stock of what has culminated in a societal moral relativism.

formation of community, followed by examining the nature of what is involved in a community and how the gospel enables a genuine community to form.

Selfishness and the Dissolution of Community

Being authorities unto ourselves is highly problematic for a community. When we all have our own ideas about what is right, we cannot agree on a common good except acceptance of everyone's self-expression. This individualism leads to a very atomized existence. Charles Taylor notes that "the dark side of individualism is a centering on the self, which both flattens and narrows our lives, makes them poorer in meaning, and less concerned with others or society."[4]

But is this a problem in the church, or is it just "out there" in the surrounding culture? I believe Carl Trueman is correct when he says, "Expressive individualism is something that affects us all. It is the very essence of the culture of which we are all a part. To put it bluntly: we are all expressive individuals now."[5] In many if not most of our churches, people decide what is good in a relativistic way. That is, what we want most is "just to be me." Even worse, this gets baptized in gospel language: "You do you . . . to the glory of God." In this way, God becomes the servant to our self-fulfillment, our self-actualization. God helps me be a better me. But this sort of pop-evangelical message isn't actually gospel. The embrace of society's individualism works against true community and is incongruent with gospel faith and practice. The call of the Christian life is to die to self. "If anyone would come after me, let him deny himself and take up his cross and follow me" (Matt. 16:24).

4. Taylor, *Ethics of Authenticity*, 4.

5. Carl R. Trueman, *The Rise and Triumph of the Modern Self: Cultural Amnesia, Expressive Individualism, and the Road to Sexual Revolution* (Crossway, 2020), 24–25.

Returning briefly to our earlier study of sin, Romans 1 sheds light on how our turning from God and his ways poisons our communities. Our active denial of the truth—our suppressing the truth in our unrighteousness (1:18)—has consequences in our relationships with others. This impacts sexuality, as men and women are given over to "dishonorable passions" and shameless acts contrary to nature (1:26–27). But it goes further, as humanity is also given over to a "debased mind to do what ought not to be done" (1:28). This expresses itself in all sorts of relational sins: covetousness, malice, envy, murder, strife, deceit, maliciousness, gossip, slander, hatred of God, insolence, pride, disobedience to parents, and all sorts of folly and faithless behavior (1:29–31). Sin is not an indifference toward the good but an active rejection of it and approval of evil (1:32). The bottom line is that sin has a deeply corrosive effect on relationships.

In view of Romans 1, it seems that the modern instantiation of "expressive individualism" is a new guise for an old problem. Beneath this commitment to self-actualization lies a deep disorder of humans seeking to choose their own order. The ego dominates, becoming the reference point for order. But as we saw earlier, sin is a choosing of one's own order against the *real* order that God has established. The folly of this choice is picked up in Proverbs. The Lord established the world in wisdom (8:22–31). The Lord delighted in this wisdom (8:30–31) and invited his people to walk in wisdom, for all who find wisdom find life, but all who hate wisdom love death (8:35–36). Sadly, in hubris, humanity continues to seek its own order for the world, living in a perpetual state of folly. This folly perpetuates the problems of our atomized existence.

Foundations of Community

It may be taken for granted that community is a good thing for humanity. From the beginning, humans have been joined to others in common purpose and truth.[6] After the fall of humanity, the need and desire for community have endured, even if it is now fraught. Societies continue to form around basic political agreements to establish a culture. These communities enable a better existence, both in cooperation and efficiency, but also in the expression of basic human characteristics. Each part of a community—the self, the neighbor, and God—sheds theological light on how communities, particularly the church, affect our lives morally.

The fact that the self poses a problem for communities, as discussed above, does not mean that the ego should be dismissed. Understanding the self is crucial to understanding any relationship to the self. In fact, the self can only be understood properly in its relations. We are who we are because of the number of relationships we have.[7] This is more than just a statement of networks but also one of morality. Our character is only known as it is demonstrable in relationship to others.

In the first instance, our self is known in relationship to our Maker. John Calvin muses about this in the introduction to his *Institutes*: "It is

6. Some have argued that relationality is integral to our being made in the image of God. For a discussion of the connection of God's relations to the imaging of God and the significance of fellowship, see Chase R. Kuhn, *The Ecclesiology of Donald Robinson and D. Broughton Knox: Exposition, Analysis, and Theological Evaluation* (Wipf & Stock, 2017), 163–67, 195–97.

7. There are a number of explorations of the notion of the self in recent academic works. A history of the modern self is treated in Trueman, *Rise and Triumph of the Modern Self.* Trueman considers a number of philosophical contributions to modern thought. Charles Taylor is one of the voices that Trueman depends on. Taylor offers one of the most sophisticated accounts of the "self" in *Sources of the Self: The Making of Modern Identity* (Harvard University Press, 1988). An interesting and informative critical interaction with Taylor's work, examining Taylor's reading of Augustine with correction, can be found in Brian Brock, *Singing the Ethos of God: On the Place of Christian Ethics in Scripture* (Eerdmans, 2005), 125–32. Brock finds much to commend in Taylor's account of the self, but wisely notes that Taylor's work is philosophy rather than theology. Brock comments that Taylor helpfully identifies longing (desire) at the heart of identity but focuses too much on "what happens *in* me," contradicting Augustine's more theological emphasis on "what happens *to* me" (131).

certain that man never achieves a clear knowledge of himself unless he has first looked upon God's face, and then descends from contemplating him to scrutinize himself. For we always seem to ourselves righteous and upright and wise and holy—this pride is innate in all of us."[8] For a human to truly understand herself, she must look to God, her Creator, who is the purest and most perfect being. Only when considering oneself in the light of God will she properly appraise her moral condition. Furthermore, it is only with a view to God that humans understand their true purpose.

But interpersonal human relationships are also instructive. We are cultured people. Since our first parents, we've always been born of a mother and father. As history has progressed, the networks of relationships have become more complex. Our identity—the notion of the "self"—is determined by relations.[9] I am a man, and I learn what it means to be a man in relationship to others. My maleness is expressed in its masculine form as I am a husband, a father, a son, a brother, a nephew, an uncle, a friend, and so forth. But more than my biological sex directing me to certain cultural participation, I also express and know my morality in each of the relationships that I keep. What love means is known and shown in each discrete context of relating. I love my wife uniquely, in a way that is different from my children but also with some similarities. I love friends or my church community differently than my nuclear family. But what would love be without any relationships? Love is not just an action but also a disposition toward others.[10] Choosing a different example,

8. John Calvin, *Institutes of the Christian Religion*, ed. John T. McNeill, trans. Ford Lewis Battles (Westminster, 1960), 1.1.2.

9. Oliver O'Donovan expresses it this way: "Persons are individuals by virtue of the given individuality of their bodies, but identities are social, and societies have no natural individual bodies. There is, then, no necessity about the form and limits of any one society over against another, and we must accept that our identities depend on something contingent and even communal." O'Donovan, *Common Objects of Love: Moral Reflection on the Shaping of Community* (Eerdmans, 2002), 42.

10. O'Donovan, *Common Objects of Love*, 16.

how would I know I am kind unless I had someone I needed to show kindness toward?

Jesus touches on the connection of oneself to others, including God, when he answers which is the greatest commandment:

> The most important is, "Hear, O Israel: The Lord our God, the Lord is one. And you shall love the Lord your God will all your heart and with all your soul and with all your mind and with all your strength." The second is this: "You shall love your neighbor as yourself." There is no other commandment greater than these. (Mark 12:28–34; cf. Matt. 22:34–40).

The core moral demand on human beings is to relate appropriately to others. Noting that we are relational people, Jesus demonstrates that a concern for others immediately follows our ultimate responsibility to God. Furthermore, our responsibility to our neighbor is tied to our understanding of and regard for self. Each of these relationships expresses a properly ordered existence: love ultimately to God as our sovereign Creator, and love unto our neighbor as unto ourselves, as a proper regard for our common kind.[11]

Virtuous Love

The demand for love needs elucidation, as what "love" is isn't immediately known. Humans express love according to what they've known or decided love should be. But this does not mean these expressions are true or best. Love requires a definition.

The apostle John wrote about the demand of love as much as any other author in the New Testament. Jesus's teaching on love, as part of

11. Augustine includes in this that proper love to neighbor will be leading one's neighbor to love God. "But as this divine Master inculcates two precepts—the love of God and the love of our neighbor—and as in these precepts a man finds three things he has to love—God, himself, and his neighbor—and that he who loves God loves himself thereby, it follows that he must endeavor to get his neighbor to love God, since he is ordered to love his neighbor as himself." Augustine, *The City of God* 19.14 (*NPNF*[1] 2:410).

his call to abide in him, forms a central part of John's record of Jesus's Farewell Discourse. Central to that section is the "new commandment" that Jesus gives to his disciples, "that you love one another: just as I have loved you, you also are to love one another" (John 13:34; cf. 15:12). This ethical challenge is grounded in a display of what true love *is*. John defines this love multiple times in his Gospel and Epistles, the clearest instances being in his First Epistle: "By this we know love, that he laid down his life for us, and we ought to lay down our lives for the brothers" (1 John 3:16; cf. John 15:13; 1 John 4:10). Every instance of this moral demand is matched with an accommodating definition grounded in the display of God's love for the world in Christ. In fact, it is because Christians are born of God and *know* God's love that they are to show the love of God to others.

It is paramount that we recognize here, once more, God's love as the source and standard of true love—much like goodness. Indeed, just as Scripture tells us "God is good" (Ps. 100:5), it also tells us "God is love" (1 John 4:8). Both love and goodness are essential to God's being. Love, therefore, has a reference and accords with true goodness. Love is from God (4:7).

God's love for the Christian community must be recognized as *the* distinctive feature of the people of God over against all other communities. Augustine defines a people group as those "bound together by common agreement as to the objects of their love." Augustine suggests that interests determine the superiority of a group of people: "It will be a superior people in proportion as it is bound together by higher interests, inferior as in proportion as it is bound together by lower."[12] This qualification of a community accords with a teleological order for existence. The highest good should be one's chief aim. Therefore, for Augustine, God being the object of a community's love establishes that community as the superior community.

12. Augustine, *City of God* 19.24 (*NPNF*[1] 2:418).

Jonathan Edwards provides a detailed exploration of love in relation to true virtue. He distinguishes between love for beings and love for the loveliness of beings.[13] He argues that virtuous love is found in goodwill toward beings rather than love for their features (such as moral excellence).[14] It is *this* love that is characteristic of God's love for his creation. Furthermore, it is love for God that must govern all other loves, as God is the Supreme Being. Edwards contends, "Love to God is most essential to true virtue; and that no benevolence whatsoever to other beings can be of the nature of true virtue without it."[15]

Edwards's teaching agrees with what is presented in the New Testament about love. God continues to be benevolent toward all people despite their disregard for him, sending sun and rain (Matt. 5:43–48). More particularly, God shows this benevolence to his redeemed people, sending his Son to die for people while they were yet sinners (Rom. 5:8). It is this sort of benevolence, which is characteristic of virtuous love, that is demanded of those who have known this love. Christ articulates this teaching in the Sermon on the Mount. He says it is not virtuous simply to love those agreeable to you, for this kind of love is common among pagans. Instead, kingdom citizens must "love your enemies and pray for those who persecute you, so that you may be sons of your Father who is in heaven" (Matt. 5:44–45).[16]

13. This belongs to a classical distinction typically employing the more technical terminology of "love of benevolence" and "love of complacence." Edwards himself used this language. The distinction between the two consists in benevolence taking no regard for the loveliness of the being, whereas complacence loves the quality of being, or its loveliness. In classic Reformed theology there is a semblance of benevolence with unconditional election.

14. Jonathan Edwards, "A Dissertation Concerning the Nature of True Virtue," in vol 1. of *The Works of Jonathan Edwards,* ed. Edward Hickman (Banner of Truth, 1974), 123.

15. Edwards, "True Virtue," 126.

16. Edwards identified the real possibility of mistaking religious activity for true virtue. True virtue emerges exclusively from God's grace. "With respect to love; it is plain by the Scripture that persons may have a kind of religious love, and yet have no saving grace. Christ speaks of many professing Christians that have such love, whose love will

The Difference Made by Gospel Grace

To show benevolent love requires a fundamental change of heart. No human being can show forth this sort of love without divine intervention. We must *know* this love before we can *show* this love. The love we're called to is unconditioned by lovely features (desirability), but is instead a general goodwill to all. It is a disposition built upon grace. When we see that we are loved so wonderfully, so fully, we are free to love others genuinely. We can love without needing something from them or justifying their worthiness of that love. Instead, we can love others simply because they are. We can seek their good, chiefly their good purposes ordered unto God. They were made by him and for him.

The gospel makes all the difference. The apostle John draws a close connection between our reception and expression of love: "We love because he first loved us" (1 John 4:19). John also appears to draw a connection between our love for others and our love for God. If we would properly love God supremely, we must love one another. "No one has ever seen God; if we love one another, God abides in us and his love is perfected in us. By this we know that we abide in him and he in us, because he has given us of his Spirit" (4:12–13). John argues that because of the indwelling of the Spirit, our regard for others is our regard for God. Therefore, as we love one another, we love God.[17] For this reason, John says that the love of God and hatred of a brother are incompatible (4:20–21).

---

not continue, and so shall fail of salvation, Matt. xxiv. 12, 13." Jonathan Edwards, *The Religious Affections* (Banner of Truth, 1961), 74.

17. This should not be mistaken as an argument for panentheism. Rather, there is a unique dynamic among Christian relationships that John builds on from Jesus's Farewell Discourse. To abide in Christ is to keep his commands. In particular, Jesus stresses love for one another as the commandment to be obeyed for abiding in him (John 13:35; 15:9–10). Furthermore, the disciples are uniquely Spirit indwelt; the Holy Spirit is the abiding presence of Christ in the life of believers.

The outcome of abiding in love is moral perfection. We are perfected in love by loving one another and thereby abiding in God (1 John 4:12, 17). Augustine marvels at God's purposes for his people, noting how our souls become more lovely by loving God. He exclaims,

> What a love must that be that makes the lover beautiful! But God is always lovely, never unlovely, never changeable. Who is always lovely first loved us; and what were we when He loved us but foul and unlovely? But not to leave us foul; no, but to change us, and of unlovely make us lovely. How shall we become lovely? By loving Him who is always lovely. As the love increases in thee, so the loveliness increases: for love is itself the beauty of the soul.[18]

In Augustine's reflections, we see the logic of God's design: God loves the unlovely to make them lovely. As the beloved know and experience God's love, they show forth the same to their neighbor. As they love genuinely, in the freedom of God's love, they become more beautiful.

Earlier, we saw the deteriorative effects of sin on the community. This damage is grounded in humanity's refusal to accept God's order for the world. In Romans 1:18–23, the impact of sin on humanity's relationship with God is expressed in false *worship*. In Romans 1:24–27, sin disorders the sexual relations of men and women, leading to dishonor in their bodies and grave consequences in the *self* (esp. v. 27, "receiving in themselves the due penalty of their error"). This "bodily" effect is repeated throughout Romans, marking the total impact of sin on life (cf. 7:24–25; 8:22–23). Finally, in Romans 1:28–32, a debased mind leads to widespread disruption of *relationships*, as people turn against one another. So, following his exposition of the gospel in Romans 1–11, the apostle Paul considers the impact

18. Augustine, *Ten Homilies on the Epistle of John* (*NPNF*[1] 7:518).

of gospel grace on believers. It should be no surprise that it leads to the undoing of the effects of sin.

Like the apostle John, Paul credits transformation to the work of God in people. In Romans 12, the ethical appeal comes through "the mercies of God" (v. 1). The call is to now present your bodies as a living sacrifice unto God, as your "reasonable" worship.[19] Here with the restoration of the self comes a call to what is sensible, proper devotion of one's whole being unto God in right worship. Furthermore, there is a call to transform the debased mind through the renewal of the mind (v. 2). No longer should believers walk in foolish ways, being "conformed to the world" (a euphemism for unrighteousness), but instead they are to discern the will of God, embracing it as good, acceptable, and perfect (v. 2). The noetic effects of the fall are undone in the newness of life in the Spirit. The renewal of the mind enables believers to no longer "suppress the truth" in their unrighteousness, living according to their own will in disobedience, but instead embrace the will of God as what is best for life. The context of change in which the renewed mind takes shape is wonderfully surprising. The immediate impact of embracing the will of God is a transformed community.

This transformation begins with a healthier view of the self. No longer should there be any pride, but instead sober judgment. Romans 12:3–8 demonstrates that there is security in gospel truth, as there is a fundamental unity in the body that mitigates any competition. Instead, there is freedom according to grace for each to exercise their gifts according to faith. A Christian's gift need not be that of another; one who exhorts need not try to be the same as the one who does acts of mercy. Collectively, these gifts function toward the good in Christ.

19. "Reasonable" is a translation of *logikēn*. I've opted for this translation over the ESV's "spiritual." BDAG renders the word "thoughtful," noting the cognitive aspect in anticipation of v. 2. The ESV acknowledges this in a footnote giving the alternative translation of "your rational service."

Recognition of an individual's place in a whole, without the threat of feeling inferior or superior, comes from the security of knowing that the whole is in Christ. Dietrich Bonhoeffer notes this foundation: "Because God has already laid the only foundation of our community, because God has united us together in one body with other Christians in Jesus Christ long before we entered into common life with them, we enter into that life together with other Christians, not as those who make demands, but as those who thankfully receive."[20] Each person's gifts and the place they hold in the community are owing entirely to Christ. Therefore, there is no competition for position or value.

Moving beyond the self, transformation affects community participation. The destructive consequences wrought by a debased mind in Romans 1:29–32 (envy, murder, strife, deceit, maliciousness, gossip, etc.) are overturned. Believers are now encouraged to "let love be genuine" (12:9). A transformed mind no longer sees others as threats to be guarded against or objects of envy or pity. Instead, there is level footing in Christ. Now there can be real honor shown to others (12:10). No longer is zeal the mark of competition, but instead of genuine appreciation for Jesus (12:11). No longer are goods something to be stored for status, but instead they can freely be given hospitably to others in need (12:13). Even one's feelings toward others are healed, as weeping and rejoicing can appropriately be expressed with others in season, where previously losses and gains for another would always threaten. Where anger and vengeance would have been responses to evil, they are now replaced with a peace that issues from a trust in the ultimate judgment of the just God (12:18–21). Once more, the transformation seen demonstrably in the community comes through the mercies of God as minds are renewed to approve God's will (12:1–2).

20. Dietrich Bonhoeffer, *Life Together and Prayerbook of the Bible*, in vol. 5 of DBW, ed. Geffrey B. Kelly, trans. Daniel W. Bloesch and James H. Burtness (Fortress, 1996), 36.

To explore this further, it is worth noting a few distinctive practices that mark out how freedom is expressed in a community bound together in Christ. Confession reminds the community that there are no self-made Christians. Rather, the fellowship's principal point of unity is that all are sinners who have been shown grace and mercy.[21] Bonhoeffer is adamant that where the community denies this, it lives a lie. "The pious community permits no one to be a sinner. Hence all have to conceal their sins from themselves and from the community. We are not allowed to be sinners. Many Christians would be unimaginably horrified if a real sinner were suddenly to turn up among the pious. So we remain alone in our sin, trapped in lies and hypocrisy, for we are in fact sinners."[22] The practice of confession occurs only where the gospel of grace is proclaimed and the worldly ways of self-righteousness are abandoned. So long as the fellowship regards one another directly, rather than in Christ, there will remain competition and independence of the most destructive kinds. Only when the people admit their utter dependence on the grace of God, regarding one another in Christ, will there be true freedom for honesty and genuine love.[23] Confession expresses the community's common problem and common source of life and love.

When there is equality in Christ, there also is the freedom for encouragement. Outside of Christ, there is only competition and insecurity. Envy is the killer of edifying encouragement. Dorothy Sayers reflects, "Envy . . . hates to see other men happy. . . . Envy is the great leveler. If it cannot level things up, it will level them down; and

21. I have in mind here especially corporate confession, although I also believe private interpersonal confession is appropriate.

22. Bonhoeffer, *Life Together*, 108.

23. Stanley Hauerwas notes, "When we exist as a forgiven people we are able to be at peace with our histories, so that now God's life determines our whole way of being—our character. We no longer need to deny our past, or tell ourselves false stories, as we now can accept what we have been without the knowledge of our sin destroying us." *The Peaceable Kingdom: A Primer in Christian Ethics*, 2nd ed. (SCM, 1983), 89.

the words constantly in its mouth are 'my rights' and 'my wrongs.' At its best, envy is a climber and a snob; at its worst, it is a destroyer; rather than have anybody happier than itself, it will see us all miserable together."[24] Envy is a mark of a debased mind, working to destroy rather than to build. If our individual merits establish our place in the community, there will be no end to rivalry and insecurity. But in Christ, there is nothing anyone could add to what is already given. Therefore, any competition is a return to worldliness. So, in Christ, there is a genuine freedom to appreciate others and offer them encouragement.[25] The body of Christ aims to be edified together through mutual words of truth spoken in love, maturing into the fullness of Christ (Eph. 4:15).

Furthermore, the security of being in Christ gives freedom to welcome others. In worldliness, a community is typically established by affinity, whether it be common activities or interests, or a mutual stage of life in society. But God's people enjoy a deeper bond. Consider again what Augustine notes about a common love—God's people enjoy a mutual love for God and one another, grounded in the love shown to them by God in Christ. This means that the Christian community, most notably the church, is not restricted to or determined by ethnicity, age, affinity, or otherwise. Indeed, those churches that are restricted by such things reflect more worldliness than gospel wisdom.

In the church, all are united in Christ, no longer regarded in worldly terms (Gal. 3:28). There is a genuine diversity among God's people who enjoy peace by the blood of Christ's cross (Eph. 2:11–22). The grand mystery of Christ is that all are welcomed as members of the body of Christ (3:6). And it is through the church, the community

24. Dorothy Sayers, "The Other Six Deadly Sins," in *Letters to a Diminished Church: Passionate Arguments for the Relevance of Christian Doctrine* (Thomas Nelson, 2004), 93.

25. Stanley Hauerwas puts it well: "In a community that has no fear of the truth, the otherness of the other can be welcomed as a gift rather than a threat." *A Community of Character: Toward a Constructive Christian Social Ethic* (University of Notre Dame Press, 1981), 50–51.

where this diverse group is joined as one body, that the wisdom of God is made known to heavenly realms and authorities (3:10). But again, this sort of community depends on gospel grace that gives all that is needed for life and enables people to freely give to others from the same source. As Bonhoeffer says, "The more genuine and the deeper our community becomes, the more everything else between us will recede, and the more clearly and purely will Jesus Christ and his work become the one and only thing that is alive between us."[26]

The Demands and Discipline of the Church

Gospel grace makes a difference to the community of God's people, and so do the gospel's demands. The gospel liberates us from the bondage of sin and the demands of the law (Rom. 6:5–14). This freedom is not for sin, but loving service (Gal. 5:13). The freedom of new life begins by the Spirit but must also be in step with the Spirit (5:25). This demands that a battle must be fought against the flesh, a euphemism for the old sinful self (5:16–17). This freedom, while being experienced in the redemption of the individual, expresses itself *in the community*. Therefore, as Paul elucidates the nature of gospel freedom, he does so with a direct view to corporate participation. The summary characteristic of life in the Spirit is love (5:14), whereas the quintessential characteristic of the flesh is conceit (5:26; cf. 5:15). Both the life of the flesh and life in the Spirit are expounded by vice and virtue lists, respectively.

Turning from the life of flesh means putting to death all vicious ways. Each evil habit that Paul specifies in Galatians 5:19–21 is grounded in the self and finds expression in the community. Pride (or conceit) takes different forms depending on the relationship. Sexual immorality, impurity, sensuality, and orgies are the sexual self being

26. Bonhoeffer, *Life Together*, 34.

expressed without restraint, using others for gratification rather than being a proper expression of love. Idolatry and sorcery are improper forms of worship, carrying the idea of manipulation and coercion for one's own ends. These undoubtedly correspond to an improper relationship with God, but there are also community implications that ought not to be missed. Idolatry and sorcery feed into community superstition, heightening tensions through coercive threats by dark spiritual practices. Interpersonal relationships are harmed by enmity, strife, jealousy, fits of anger, rivalries, dissensions, divisions, and envy as the ego is at war with neighbors. Each of these characteristics shows the self in battle against others, seeking self-justification. Finally, drunkenness is a life out of control. In all these vicious habits—the works of the flesh—the ego is the dominant problem. The demand of the new life in Christ is death to the old self. "I have been crucified with Christ. It is no longer I who live, but Christ who lives in me. And the life I now live in the flesh I live by faith in the Son of God, who loved me and gave himself for me" (Gal. 2:20).

The newness of life in the Spirit carries with it positive demands. Not only are the vicious old ways of the flesh to be ungratified but the desires of the Spirit are meant to be pursued wholeheartedly (Gal. 5:16–17). Desire is an important moral concept. Genuine desire, or our deepest love, is only properly oriented when our hearts have turned to God in faith. The apostle Paul makes this clear in his appeal to Timothy: "The aim of our charge is love that issues from a pure heart and a good conscience and a sincere faith" (1 Tim. 1:5). True love, the summarizing characteristic of life in the Spirit, comes from sincere faith. This faith is gospel trust that dispels all uncertainty and insecurity, giving the believer a pure heart and good conscience. In this freedom, the believer engages the community with virtue that comes from the Spirit working in the heart. Love, joy, peace, patience, kindness, goodness, faithfulness, gentleness, and self-control are all habits formed in gospel freedom. They are the result of a life that has "crucified the flesh with its passions and desires" (Gal. 5:24).

The opposition of the life of the flesh and life in the Spirit is not static. There is an ongoing tension between the two that continues until the perfection of the believer at the coming of Christ (Rom. 8, esp. vv. 10–11). This means that the Christian community is a crucible for character transformation.[27] Paul expects that believers will continue to battle with sin, and therefore the community of the church are to hold one another to account. Mutual accountability is in service of spiritual restoration, always conducted in a spirit of gentleness (Gal. 6:1). But there is always an implicit danger of the ego exploiting a brother or sister's weakness and vulnerability. The apostle warns believers not to fall into temptation during such times. Instead, as believers bear one another's burdens, they are to do so in love, fulfilling the law of Christ (6:2). The time of mutual accountability is not a platform for overcoming another, proving some notion of superiority or dominance, but instead a common recognition of a mutual ongoing battle with the flesh, taking shape in distinct ways in each one's life. This battle is not one for comparison or competition (6:4), as envy and provocation of one another are owing to conceit (5:26) and not the new life in the Spirit.

Imitation is important in the community. Habits are formed not just by self-discipline but by learning from the example of others. Indeed, the moral life is certainly intellectual, but it is more. Morality is not formed simply through indoctrination but through a community of examples of life lived according to truth. Paul instructs the Philippians, "Brothers [and sisters], join in imitating me, and keep your eyes on those who walk according to the example you have in us" (Phil. 3:17). Later, Paul adds a remark about this life of imitation, showing it isn't according to subjective standards but according to the truth:

27. I will consider challenges external to the community of faith in the next chapter.

"What you have learned and received and heard and seen in me—practice these things, and the God of peace will be with you" (4:9). This charge of imitation with a view to peace is in the context of interpersonal conflict in the Philippian congregation. Paul admonishes them to stick to what they know to be true (4:1) and to rejoice always in these things (4:4). It is only when there is a reversion to worldly concerns that the community is fractured. But the life habituated in gospel truth knows peace.

The community that shares life in the Spirit eschews earthly things as kingdom citizens (Phil. 3:19–20). The allure of worldly comfort or merit is a constant threat to believers, but in the community of faith, there is a constant reminder of gospel truth: All that the world would value as gain for self-righteousness and status is counted as rubbish for the sake of knowing Christ and his righteousness (3:2–11). Indeed, this life of dependence and faith is not a solo effort but a community habit. Christians congregate to celebrate and remind one another of their common life in Christ. The destruction of the congregation is the return to worldly appraisal and security (3:18–19), looking around at one another to form a religious pecking order. But the vibrant and vivacious church community fixes their gaze on the One who is the model of humility and self-sacrifice (2:5–11), holding true to that common possession and love (3:14).

Imitation is not one-dimensional, as it requires multiple generations to impart truth and wisdom to one another. It comes through direct instruction as well as observation. Wisdom is disseminated to the community through the generations. In the Proverbs, the father's instruction to the son leads to knowledge and understanding. The call to the young man (the son) is to heed the commandments, wisdom, and instruction so as to avoid folly.[28] This sort of instruction

28. For instance, Prov. 1:8; 2:1; 3:1, 21; 4:1, 10, 20; 5:1, 7; 6:20; 7:1, 24 are a father addressing a son with the admonition to keep his father's commandment and the words of his mouth. This admonition also includes the teaching of the son's mother (6:20). Throughout

is to begin in the home (cf. Deut. 6:1–9; Eph. 6:1–4; 2 Tim. 1:5; 3:14–15), but it also belongs to the broader community of faith. In the church, the relationships with other believers become like family. Older men are to be encouraged as fathers, younger men as brothers, older women as mothers, and younger women as sisters (1 Tim. 5:1–2). These relationships do not cancel the responsibility for biological family (5:3–8) but instead govern the ways of relating to others in the church. These relationships are not unidirectional but honor *both* young and old, recognizing the significance of all. Modeling may begin with the habits of the older generations, but they are expected to be cultivated in the younger generations (Titus 2:1–6). Young leaders are not to be despised because of their age, but instead are challenged to be examples themselves—as was Timothy in Ephesus—in their words, works, and attitudes (1 Tim. 4:11–16; cf. Titus 2:7–8).[29]

Leadership plays an important role in one final dimension of community life: discipline. This work is not exclusive to the leadership (eldership) of the church, but they hold an authoritative role of responsibility for proper discipline of members to maintain life according to gospel faith. Jesus provides a basic system of church discipline in Matthew 18:15–20. The aim of this system was reconciliation and repentance. Just prior to this, Jesus teaches about the appropriateness of humility for kingdom citizens and the danger of pride (18:1–4). He also warns of the severe consequences for those who lead others to temptation and those who succumb to temptation (18:5–9); sin carries the consequence of hell fire (v. 9). Jesus makes it clear that

---

the remainder of the Proverbs, this sort of generational instruction is crucial (e.g., 10:1; 13:1; 15:5; 16:31; 17:25; 19:18, 26–27; 20:29; 22:6, 15, 28; 23:22–26; 24:21; 28:7; 30:17; 31:26–28).

29. Elsewhere, I've challenged the homogeneity of age-specific ministries. See Chase R. Kuhn, "The Doctrine of the Church and Age-Specific Ministries," in *Australian Evangelical Perspectives on Youth Ministry: Identity, Church, Culture, and Discipleship*, ed. Ruth Lukabyo (Wipf & Stock, 2023), 63–85.

the will of God is for his "little ones" to live, meaning that he desires repentance from sin when they are lost.

In this context, Jesus teaches his disciples about discipline within the church. Sin is to be treated in a manner that seeks repentance and reconciliation. Offense is to be treated among as few people as necessary, only escalating when a sinner refuses to listen, acknowledge sin, and repent. Only if there is an utter refusal to turn away from sin when finally brought before the church is the person to be treated as an unbeliever (Matt. 18:17). The leadership in these situations exercise the "keys of the kingdom" (cf. 16:19), binding and loosing in a manner that accords with the truth of the gospel (18:18).[30] Following this teaching, Jesus provides a parable warning against unforgiveness (18:21–35). Disciplining others demonstrates the accordance of community life with gospel faith in both its condemnation of sin and its offer of forgiveness.

Discipline, therefore, holds two concerns together: one for the individual caught in sin and one for the church impacted by the sinner. The apostle Paul makes this clear in his First Epistle to the Corinthians. He challenges the congregation not to tolerate unrepentant sin in the church, commanding the church "to deliver this man to Satan for the destruction of the flesh, so that his spirit may be saved in the day of the Lord" (1 Cor. 5:4–5). The first concern is saving the sinner, even through tough discipline. But the second concern follows: "Do you not know that a little leaven leavens the whole lump?"

30. The use of the "keys" was a significant matter leading to the Reformation. Martin Luther's treatise "The Keys" challenged papal abuse of power and misuse of the keys. Luther argued that the church did more binding than loosing, used loosing for profits (indulgences), claimed secret knowledge of what was bound in heaven, and was hypocritical in the use of the keys, applying it to people but not to ecclesiastical powers. Luther contends that the keys were meant to be a gift for the church, as absolution was proclaimed. See Luther, "The Keys," *LW* 40, 320–77. The practice of absolution to accompany corporate confession became a standard fixture in Protestant liturgies (e.g., Anglican Book of Common Prayer Communion Service).

(5:6). The toleration of sin has a tainting effect on the congregation. Far from being "somebody else's business," it is the concern of the community to root out evil from their midst (5:13). This sin will not always require expulsion of the sinner, but it will always require the attention of the people who have been delivered from sin through Christ's sacrifice (5:7).

The joint concern for individuals and the community makes the Lord's Supper the activity where discipline is most often practiced. Word and sacrament have been the definitive marks in Protestant churches since the Reformation, but many traditions adopted discipline as a third mark of the church early on.[31] Discipline was seen as an extension of the ministry of Word and sacrament, as the right reception of both should lead believers to godly living. However, when the order is denied in the life of the believer, discipline is necessary for correction. The natural place for this practice to be expressed is in the communion meal. The apostle Paul instructs the church about the need for self-examination regarding sin when joining together for the Lord's Supper, cautioning the congregation that eating and drinking in an unworthy manner will bring judgment upon oneself (1 Cor. 11:27–32). Paul's warning is against individual sin as well as against discord in the community. The communion meal is a central activity to the life of the church, reminding the congregation of their fundamental unity in Christ and the new life they enjoy together in him. If believers are not living in unity or not walking in the newness of life, then personal abstinence or enforced exclusion from the meal should lead the believer to repentance. They do not come to the table because of their own righteousness; instead, they come appreciating

31. Calvin understands discipline to be necessary in the church because of Christ's teaching and the apostles' teaching, but he does not number it as a mark of the church, which he reserves for preaching of the Word and the right administration of the sacraments. He does, however, see discipline as necessary for the good of the church (*Institutes* 4.12).

the righteousness given to them in Christ. Ongoing unrepentant sin and discord are not an appreciation of Christ's sacrifice.

Conclusion

Repentance of sin and regular community participation in love are the programs for God's people in this age. The church is the place for God's people to be formed and to mature morally. This formation is not one-dimensional, as we have seen, but instead requires growth in knowledge, discernment, cultivation of virtue, loving service, humility, and forgiveness. In fact, this formation is better understood as transformation. It is the renewal of life, now lived in the Spirit, putting off the old self and its fleshly desire and walking in the newness of life, becoming more like Christ (Col. 3:1–17). As we have seen, this life is not restricted to individuals but is lived out in a community. Forgiveness is central to the demonstration of love in the community, reassuring believers of the gospel's truth and power.[32] Christ himself insists that if his followers are to abide in him, it would be through their love for one another (John 15:1–17; cf. 1 John 3:23–24).

There is a wonderful consequence of love in the community: God's love is known and shown. Augustine showed us that through participation in love, God's people are transformed into more beautiful people. Beautification is preparatory, priming the church for Christ's return (Phil. 1:9–11; Titus 2:11–14). In fact, this participation in love has the wonderfully comforting effect of reassuring believers of their place in Christ. As Christians are being transformed, even

32. Andrew Errington notes forgiveness is distinctive of Christian ethics. "Faith's active impulse is always already oriented in a certain direction, because it is only ever experienced as forgiveness. The faith that is formed by love is already oriented by the form in which it has arisen: through being forgiven." *Every Good Path: Wisdom and Practical Reason in Christian Ethics and the Book of Proverbs* (T&T Clark, 2020), 189. See also Errington, "Forgiveness and the Novelty of Christian Ethics," *Modern Theology* 39, no. 3 (July 2023): 472–89.

through recognition of sin and mortifying the flesh, they grow in confidence in the Spirit's work in them. Only in the church community is this transformation truly tested and known. The apostle John tells us God's will: "And this is his commandment, that we believe in the name of his Son Jesus Christ and love one another, just as he commanded us. Whoever keeps his commandments abides in God, and God in him. And by this we know that he abides in us, by the Spirit whom he has given us" (1 John 3:23–24). Loving participation in the community gives believers confidence that they will not be unprepared to meet Christ on the day of his return (1 John 2:28–29). We turn in our next and final chapter to this life lived in anticipation of Christ's return.

9

The End of Ethics

The Good Life in Eschatological Perspective

For the grace of God has appeared, bringing salvation for all people, training us to renounce ungodliness and worldly passions, and to live self-controlled, upright, and godly lives in the present age, waiting for our blessed hope, the appearing of the glory of our great God and Savior Jesus Christ, who gave himself for us to redeem us from all lawlessness and to purify for himself a people for his own possession who are zealous for good works.

Titus 2:11–14

Here surely is an answer to your question as to what is the starting-point, and what is the goal: we begin in faith, and are made perfect by sight. This is also the sum of the whole body of doctrine.[1]

Saint Augustine

1. Augustine, from chap. 5 of *Enchiridion* (*NPNF*[1] 3:238).

Good mysteries create intrigue by revealing enough details to keep you waiting eagerly for the end. In fact, the end is often known from the beginning: what was the crime, the mode of the crime, and perhaps even the time of the crime. But there is always a question around certain key details that keeps the audience engaged attentively, waiting for the end. Christian eschatology is much like this, knowing the end before it occurs, but some key details are purposefully omitted to keep believers engaged. We confess in faith that Christ will come again to judge the living and the dead, but we do not know the day or the hour. The call of the Christian in this age is to wait watchfully.

Waiting is one of the most difficult things for humans to do. Patience truly is a virtue. But the problem is especially acute when you are waiting for your life and happiness; this is the life of faith. "For you have died, and your life is hidden with Christ in God. When Christ who is your life appears, then you also will appear with him in glory" (Col. 3:3–4). Our life and happiness is Christ, and we wait for him. As we wait, we're aware of the trials Jesus warns of and the hope we have: "In the world you will have tribulation. But take heart; I have overcome the world" (John 16:33). Jesus's words are a promise that demands faith. In this life, in this world, we have hope even as we face challenges. Hence the Christian life is often identified as one of tension, a life of already and not yet.

In the previous chapter, I considered how the present time of life in the church is for the Christian's moral formation. In this chapter, I affirm the Christian life is in tension with the world. This tension, too, is for the believer's moral formation; the life of faith, lived in hope, is one of moral expectation that demands love. But this love is not a love of the world or the things of the world (1 John 2:15). Instead, it is a love of God that orders our engagement with the world. According to John Webster, this amounts to a life of "passive activity and active passivity, 'waiting for and hastening the coming day of God.'

And why? Because the truth of our situation is that we are those who occupy that place in history where the most truthful thing to do is this: 'according to his promise [to] wait for new heavens and a new earth in which righteousness dwells' (2 Pet. 3.11–13)."[2]

My aim in this chapter is to demonstrate that the promise of Christ's coming confirms the teleological order of the creation, and therefore that ethics are inherently eschatological. I hope this conviction will promote an expectant moral existence for Christians who await Christ's return. We will begin with a brief account of the relationship between ethics and eschatology. Then, we will consider the life of *faith* that frames both significance and suffering in this life. Next, we will explore how *hope* tempers our political participation in society, looking ahead to the transformation and renewal that Christ will enact. And finally, we will examine a life of *love* as both fitting now and for eternity.

The End of All Things

To offer any meaningful account of ethics, there must be a teleological order, a purposefulness to action and being. When considering human agency, no act or way of relating to the world would have significance apart from a given order. Life would simply, and quite literally, be meaningless; this has been my contention throughout this book. But here I wish to uncover the unique contribution of Christian theology to ethics: The world was created with purpose by the sovereign Creator, and his ongoing purpose is displayed in the advent of Jesus Christ. Furthermore, the first advent of Jesus announced to the world God's eschatological purposes, which will be fully and finally revealed at the second advent of Christ. This context—the

2. John Webster, "Eschatology and Anthropology," in *Word and Church: Essays in Christian Dogmatics* (T&T Clark, 2001), 286.

salvation-historical narrative of human origin and destiny—frames ethics, giving meaning to agency. "That drama is the space of our action, the field within which what we do is possible and meaningful."[3]

It is important to recognize the shared moral field we inhabit with the world of the Bible. This *is* God's world, and we live in the same shared history as the world of the Scriptures. Crucially, the order of the world as it was created has been affirmed as something good in God's sending his Son to redeem that order. God has planned for and promised a future for *this* world, even if it will be transformed and perfected as a *new* heavens and earth. Central to this purpose, and to all of history, is Jesus Christ. It was by and for the Son that all things were created (Col 1:16). Even now, it is in him that all things hold together (1:17). Furthermore, it is through him that all things will be reconciled to God both on earth and in heaven (1:20). Nowhere is this testified to more clearly than in the resurrection of Christ, where the triumph and endurance of goodness are proclaimed. And so, we return to where we began: Jesus is the beginning and end of morality.

The "day of the Lord" is an important motif in Scripture, capturing the eschatological nature of ethics. The coming of this day represents accountability and revelation, unveiling the true nature of the world by the sovereign Lord in order to bring justice and judgment. That this day exists in the future has long tempted the people of God and the wider world to deny that it will ever occur, thus judging morality as insignificant and relative. Even the leaders of God's people have at times proclaimed, "Everyone who does evil is good in the sight of the Lord, and he delights in them"; they have questioned, "Where is the God of justice?" (Mal. 2:17). Some have exploited the delay in the Lord's judgment, using it as an excuse for hedonistic indulgence (2 Pet. 2). Their justification for their sin has come through the mocking question, "Where is the promise of his coming? For ever since the fathers

3. Webster, "Eschatology and Anthropology," 283.

fell asleep, all things are continuing as they were from the beginning of creation" (2 Pet 3:4). Yet in Malachi and Peter's prophetic words, that day is delayed to give opportunity for repentance. Judgment's delay is not because it won't come but because it is *so certain*; God is giving an opportunity for sinners even now to return to him. "The Lord is not slow to fulfill his promise as some count slowness, but is patient toward you, not wishing that any should perish, but that all should reach repentance" (2 Pet. 3:9; cf. Mal. 3:6–7).

Therefore, the end of all things will be revealed at the end of time. It is known now because God has made it known. But it remains, for now, an object of faith. The moral life is the life aligned to this proper end, lived by faith in the Son of God. In this world, faith will contend with sight, ever tempted to relativize life to the immediate rather than the eternal. But the Spirit's presence brings power and is the eschatological reality of eternal life breaking through in this present moment, seeing believers through to their proper end in Christ. We now move to consider how faith features in our moral experience awaiting the end of all things.

Faith

Ethically, faith serves a causal purpose in our righteousness.[4] In other words, faith is how righteousness comes to believers. The significance of this point can be seen in two differing translations of Romans 1:17: (a) "the righteous will live by faith," and (b) "the righteous by faith will live." The second of these is the preferable translation, aligning with Paul's emphasis throughout his writings that justification is

4. In Greek, there are several ways to express that righteousness that comes "by" or "through" faith. The two common prepositions, respectively, are *ek* and *dia*, both typically in the genitive form. These words express a causal or instrumental relationship of faith to righteousness. For example, Rom. 3:22, "the righteousness of God through [*dia*] faith in Jesus Christ for all who believe." BDAG identifies this use of *dia* as a "marker of instrumentality," specifically denoting an "efficient cause." Entry 3d under "διά."

by faith.[5] This subtle difference of emphasis shifts the focus morally from righteousness awarded for a life lived a certain way to life given because righteousness is awarded for dependence on another.

But though righteousness is by faith, faith will certainly "work" and have a bearing on the life of the believer. The apostle James argues, "Faith by itself, if it does not have works, is dead" (James 2:17). Faith will be demonstrable in the life of the Christian. Claiming faith and living otherwise does not represent true faith. And so, our exploration of faith in view of the end of all things is an exploration of true dependence on Christ for righteousness. The most noteworthy biblical themes for the life lived in faith may be categorized as *significance* and *suffering*.

Significance

Citizenship in the kingdom of heaven reframes one's conception of significance. Disciples of Christ are not preoccupied with the concerns of this life in the same way as unbelievers. Jesus taught that one of the great blocks to the Word of God growing and flourishing in life is the "cares of the world and the deceitfulness of riches" (Matt. 13:22), the thorns that choke the Word and make its growth unfruitful. We might broadly consider these cares and riches under the banner of significance—that is, what we regard as important and providing security. Faith leads Christians to have a different perspective, finding security and meaning beyond temporal matters. Knowing God as one's heavenly Father provides reassurance that all that is needed will be supplied (Matt. 6:25–32; cf. Luke 12:22–34); even if this life should expire, God has given his only Son to provide believers with eternal life (John 3:16).

Jesus knew the temptations of worldly significance and comfort. When the Holy Spirit led him into the desert to be tempted by the

5. For a clear and persuasive exposition of why faith (*pistis*) should be understood as an objective genitive in Rom. 3:22, and in Rom. 1:17 (following Hab. 2:4), see Frank Thielman, *Romans*, ZECNT (Zondervan Academic, 2018), 204–5, cf. 81–84.

devil, he was challenged with three temptations. In the first, the devil challenged Jesus, hungry from fasting, to turn stones into loaves of bread. Jesus rebuffed the devil with words of a better perspective: "Man shall not live by bread alone, but by every word that comes from the mouth of God" (Matt. 4:4; cf. Deut. 8:3). In the second, the devil challenged Jesus to "do something spectacular, something that could win him great applause."[6] But not needing to prove himself, Jesus refused to throw himself from the temple in demonstration of his identity. Instead, he responded, "Again it is written, 'You shall not put the Lord your God to the test'" (Matt. 4:7; cf. Deut. 6:16). Likewise, in the third temptation, the devil took Jesus to a high mountain and showed him the kingdoms of the earth and their glory. The devil offered Jesus the kingdoms of the world if Jesus would fall down and worship him. Again, with a better perspective on significance, Jesus replied, "You shall worship the Lord your God and him only shall you serve" (Matt. 4:10; cf. Deut. 6:13).

In all three of Jesus's responses to the devil, he demonstrates a proper understanding of significance grounded in teleology. In all three temptations, the offers themselves were not materially bad, but they were evil when in exchange for a proper teleological order. Jesus demonstrated that faith in God's provision of satisfaction is better than immediate gratification. Faith believes in God's Word irrespective of circumstantial needs or desires. In his temptations, the Lord Jesus recapitulated the temptations of Israel to sacrifice faith for things they deemed more immediately (or ultimately) significant, and in his obedience, he provided a way for God's people to be righteous.

The temptations of worldly cares are not simply subjective, internal challenges for locating significance, but also the message of the world

6. Henri J. M. Nouwen, *In the Name of Jesus: Reflections on Christian Leadership* (Crossroad, 1989), 53.

seeking objective significance, which creates hostility to believers. In his Farewell Discourse, Jesus warns of this: "If the world hates you, know that it has hated me before it hated you. If you were of the world, the world would love you as its own; but because you are not of the world, but I chose you out of the world, therefore the world hates you" (John 15:18–19). Life in Christ is a life of ultimate significance, over against the penultimate things the world clings to, and by this new identity the world is confronted and exposed.

Jesus says, "I am the light of the world" (John 9:5). This light brings hope for those who will walk in it but threatens the darkness. Therefore, the call of faith is to trust in the light, knowing "the darkness has not overcome it" (1:4). In fact, quite the opposite, Jesus has "overcome the world" (16:33). Amidst the tribulation of life in the world, Jesus promises peace. This peace comes in the form not of something abstract but of someone personal—the Holy Spirit. "For everyone who has been born of God overcomes the world. And this is the victory that has overcome the world—our faith" (1 John 5:4). As Christians sojourn in this life in the power of the Holy Spirit, they do so in the confidence that, by faith, they have overcome the world in Christ.

The call to faith is presented not only with a promise but also a severe command: "Do not love the world or the things of this world" (1 John 2:15). The reason is provided: "If anyone loves the world, the love of the Father is not in him. For all that is in the world—the desires of the flesh and the desires of the eyes and the pride of life—is not from the Father but from the world. And the world is passing away along with its desires, but whoever does the will of God abides forever" (2:15–17). This is the heart of the life of faith lived in eschatological tension. The world is morally opposed to God. Therefore, all the world's desires, which promise a lasting sense of significance, are false trails. The apostle James makes it clear in a rhetorical question: "Do you not know that friendship with the world is enmity with

God?" (James 4:4). This question of loyalty presents a challenging moral position to disciples of Christ; they must always remember where real significance is found. "Whoever loves his life loses it, and whoever hates his life in this world will keep it for eternal life" (John 12:25). The world is not a place of comfort for the disciple, but of sojourning in faith as we await Christ our life to appear.

Suffering

Far from being a journey of peace, the life of discipleship is guaranteed strife. The challenges far exceed the temptation to worldliness, including suffering because of resistance to the world's ways. The darkness despises the light, and therefore those who walk in the light will be hated by the world. This is one of the great tensions of the eschatological age: living life content with discomfort. By faith, disciples follow Christ even to the grave, knowing that death has been overcome by Christ who went before them.

The expectation of suffering is one of the frequent motifs in the New Testament. Jesus and the apostles after him taught that affliction was to be expected by kingdom citizens. In his Sermon on the Mount, Jesus clearly links the expectation of suffering and morality: "Blessed are those who are persecuted for righteousness' sake, for theirs is the kingdom of heaven" (Matt. 5:10). This righteousness is defined as the cause of Christ in the verses that follow. "Blessed are you when others revile you and persecute you and utter all kinds of evil against you falsely on my account. Rejoice and be glad, for your reward is great in heaven, for so they persecuted the prophets before you" (5:11–12). Righteousness does not bear an immediate reward of comfort but is pursued by faith. The immediate return for righteous living is the abuse of the world in verbal, social, and/or physical assaults. Faith recognizes that righteousness is not a strategy for worldly gain but for heavenly security.

The apostle Peter makes much of Jesus's teaching on persecution in both of his epistles. He opens his first letter with a declaration of praise to God for "an inheritance that is imperishable, undefiled, and unfading, kept in heaven" (1 Pet. 1:3–4). This reminder is for those who "by God's power are being guarded through faith for a salvation ready to be revealed in the last time" (1:5). The future vision of security—something God himself is assuring—encourages those who live amidst present trials. These present challenges serve a refining purpose—testing and proving the genuineness of faith (1:6–7). In an atmosphere of hostility, believers demonstrate their confidence in things unseen, things they wait for by faith.

As believers live life waiting for the return of Christ, Peter instructs them to be holy (1 Pet. 1:15). While sojourning in life, honorable conduct will be a witness to the world, even if not until the final day (2:12). Doing good and suffering for it is a gracious thing in the sight of God (2:20), the calling of believers after the example of Christ (2:21), who suffered sinlessly unto death (2:22–25). To return to the world's ways—exchanging evil for evil or indulging the desires of the flesh—would be a mockery of Christ's sacrifice, who bore our sins so "that we might die to sin and live to righteousness" (2:24). The death of sin in the life of the believer is enacted through suffering, as faith puts to death worldly desires.

In this way, suffering is not merely external, through the persecution of the world, but also internal as the Spirit overcomes the flesh: "Whoever has suffered in the flesh has ceased from sin so as to live the rest of the time in the flesh no longer for human passions but for the will of God" (1 Pet. 4:1–2). It is not difficult to see why faith is so integral to this suffering, for the endurance of discomfort is not natural. Human beings long for peace and comfort. Faith stresses that there is comfort to be found, but not yet. It is known now only through belief in a future day when it will be revealed. For now, suffering is intended for joy, not in a masochistic way but in anticipation of the rejoicing that will be known at the glorious appearance of Christ (4:13).

Faith, then, demands endurance of suffering. Faith commits itself to a reality not yet known, as the life of suffering is the blessed life (Matt. 5:11; 1 Pet. 4:14). But in another way, faith produces endurance. Faith amidst trial brings about the perfection of the Christian life. When faith is tested, it creates steadfastness, and this—when it has run its course—results in completion (James 1:2–4). The apostle Paul captures this course in life as the joy of justification by faith. By faith, believers are given the grace to stand and rejoice in the hope of the glory of God (Rom. 5:1–2). This grace leads believers to "rejoice in our sufferings, knowing that suffering produces endurance, and endurance produces character, and character produces hope, and hope does not put us to shame, because God's love has been poured into our hearts through the Holy Spirit who has been given to us" (5:3–5). Suffering in faith is God's plan for believers' perfection. Trials are the crucible in which moral character is formed. Therefore, in hope, believers should rejoice in suffering, knowing that God uses even difficult and painful things for good. Look no further than the cross for assurance.

Hope

Hope is the vision of the life lived in faith. Faith proceeds in the assurance of realities yet to be revealed, things hoped for presently. This hope generates a certain contentment in the present life, tempering action and shaping character in the promise of what is coming. Hope is not hollow, wishful thinking that imagines away the worries of this life. Hope is personal, focused on Jesus amidst present struggles. All that we long for is fulfilled in Jesus. He is our hope. He is our future.

Therefore, a life lived in eschatological tension must wait in hope. Hope is the moral posture of faith, curtailing the efforts Christians may be tempted to make to realize the kingdom before its time. No doubt, the kingdom has been inaugurated, and we enjoy the guarantee of its future in the presence of the Holy Spirit (Rom. 8:23; Gal. 5:5). But there is a danger of demanding more than we're assured at this moment—what is commonly referred to as "over-realized eschatology." While we wait for the appearing of Christ, in our impatience we can seek to execute justice of our own, to deliver judgment on God's behalf, to take the world through political force, to deny the power structures of temporal governments, to dismiss the value of the present, or to transform the world through cultural activities. Hope demands an ethical patience that waits expectantly for the consummation of the kingdom, something that Christ will bring when he returns. This section will briefly explore several significant areas of life where hope shapes our present moral experience.[7]

Justice and Judgment

Injustice sits at the heart of unrest. While evil remains unpunished, while that which is bad is called good, while atrocities are tolerated and even encouraged, there can be no peace. We have already considered the nature of sin in an earlier chapter, but it is worth noting once more that our unrest in the world emerges from our choice of an alternative order for our lives.[8] Strife with humanity comes from that cursed postlapsarian state where humanity is no longer seen as my kind, but instead as my enemy and a threat to my security. Though

7. The themes treated here are typically considered political theology. This section is very concise, at risk of being scant. For an excellent and much fuller treatment of these themes and more, consider David VanDrunen, *Politics After Christendom: Political Theology in a Fractured World* (Zondervan Academic, 2020).

8. Oliver O'Donovan notes, "We can determine ourselves as we are determined, or we can determine ourselves in defiance of our determination. We can either be just or unjust—not that these are equal alternatives in an ontological sense, since injustice is ultimately unreality; but they are alternatives practically, as deliberative possibilities." *The Ways of Judgment* (Eerdmans, 2005), 31.

the world remains cursed at present, it does not mean that justice is a worthless pursuit. Common order in a civil domain depends upon systems of justice. While these will never bring the ultimate justice that will come at the parousia, temporal justice is a good cause. At the heart of any system of justice, there must be a good system of valuation.[9]

A notion of equality is foundational to good valuation of human life in comparison with other created goods. There must be some way of distinguishing kinds. Oliver O'Donovan is correct when he says, "The equality of all human beings cannot simply be posited . . . it has to be grounded in a truth that is to be told about humankind's relations to that which is not humankind, and the only relation which answers the point is that in which each human being stands to the creator."[10] VanDrunen believes that this foundational system of equality was preserved after the fall in God's covenant with Noah (Gen. 8:14–9:17, esp. 9:1–7).[11] There God reaffirmed the value of human life in a rudimentary system of justice, giving the law of retaliation (*lex talionis*; Gen. 9:6) in demonstration of the worth of each individual human in relation to their own and other kinds. This universal covenant with creation abides as part of God's common grace in the world, serving cultural systems of order (e.g., human law) that seek to maintain just societies.

However, temporal systems of justice are always fraught because of the people administering judgment. God alone is omnipotent, possessing true knowledge of the moral character of actions. Jesus is "he who searches mind and heart, and will give to each of [them] according to [their] works" (Rev. 2:23). Therefore, while a jury of

9. For theological treatments of systems of justice, see O'Donovan, *Ways of Judgment*, 31–51; VanDrunen, *Politics After Christendom*, 249–89.

10. O'Donovan, *Ways of Judgment*, 41

11. David VanDrunen, *Divine Covenants and Moral Order: A Biblical Theology of Natural Law* (Eerdmans, 2014), 95–132.

peers or an educated and experienced judge may preside in making judgments against human affairs, no human judgment is guaranteed a complete account of the facts. Human judgments are limited by their finitude. Furthermore, there is always the possibility of the intrusion of bias in judgments when those judging use their position to achieve unjust ends. Some lands contend for the "right" of freedom of religion or speech, but these are tested by other "rights" that may be infringed by moral judgments (e.g., sexuality, gender roles, identity, social well-being). I cannot address these concerns at length here, but it is worth mentioning how this societal struggle with justice affects the Christian moral experience.

Christians must seek to demonstrate the value and dignity of all human life across differences of ethnicity, religion, gender, or otherwise. Contending for the dignity of life, from birth to death, across all social groups is a testament to God's good preservation of the world. Christians should make this claim publicly, even without reference to a direct theological rationale.[12] But this advocacy will not bring about the kingdom. It will testify to God's good provision for the world but will not change the world in a lasting way. The human heart remains the problem; therefore, true peace and justice will come only when evil is finally judged. Justice remains, therefore, an object of hope.

But within the church, there must be justice and proper judgment. A vision for justice begins with a reconfiguring of social relationships with respect to Christ. "For as many of you were baptized into Christ have put on Christ. There is neither Jew nor Greek, there is neither

12. What I mean is that contending for this good is something common and can be appealed to in common terms. Though theological reason may not be necessary or even appropriate, there remains good theological reason all the same. For this sort of social action, appeals may most effectively be made along the lines of natural law. This being said, I agree with Duncan Forrester that "human beings are to be treated with respect because they are of equal worth, independently of their ability, contribution, success, work or desert. . . . But it is difficult to see how this core affirmation can be justified without theological reference." *On Human Worth* (SCM, 2001), 30–31.

slave nor free, there is no male and female, for you are all one in Christ Jesus" (Gal. 3:27–28). Baptism into Christ is what secures equality as a foundation of just treatment in the church. But this belonging does not mean there is no judgment. Because all are in Christ, the community has no tolerance for sin. In 1 Corinthians 5 (esp. vv. 9–13), Paul makes a strong statement about the necessity of judgment *in* the church, leading to a disassociation with the unrepentant. But Paul remarks that this judgment and disassociation is not expected for relations with those *outside* the church.

The actions and restrictions related to judgment are all in view of the coming end when Christ will judge the world. The church acts to bring judgment among believers in preparation for Christ. Indeed, judgment begins with the house of God (1 Pet. 4:16–19); therefore, believers must be encouraged to do good. However, the judgment in the church is not harsh but predicated on the work of Christ, marked by forgiveness. Therefore, the administration of justice is in pursuit of ongoing peace in the reconciliation won at the cross. Retaliation and retribution are withheld from other believers because of their mutual standing in grace (Matt. 5:38–42). Even enemies must be loved (5:43–48). Sins are not dismissed as insignificant nor left unaddressed, but are treated always in view of an ultimate judgment. Likewise, the church's judgment of outsiders is withheld in any ultimate sense, knowing that that day is coming. For now, believers live as ambassadors of Christ, exercising the ministry of reconciliation (2 Cor. 5:16–21). In Jesus, "God was reconciling the world to himself, not counting their trespasses against them" (5:19). So, while judgment may be withheld, believers implore the world to "be reconciled to God" (5:20).

This view of justice reframes the kind of experience that believers now endure in the world. Christian hope longs for the judgment of the world but does so with a felt tension. On the one hand, there is a deep yearning for wrongs to be made right. Those who have misled the world in deception, agents of Satan, along with those who have persecuted the faithful, those who have abused power in the world and carried out violence and injustice—all of these will be judged and brought to final justice. This day will be glorious, even if gruesome, as the Lord will be seen to be just. Cries of praise will accommodate the destruction of the wicked. "Hallelujah! Salvation and glory and power belong to our God, for his judgments are true and just; for he has judged the great prostitute who corrupted the earth with her immorality and has avenged on her the blood of his servants" (Rev. 19:1–2). In hope, then, we can see "evidence of the righteous judgment of God" in our suffering for the kingdom, expecting the execution of justice that will come with the revelation of Christ (2 Thess. 1:5–12). But on the other hand, we hope for judgment with solemnity, knowing it will be final. When judgment comes, there will be no more opportunity for repentance of sin, no more calls to turn to the Lord. And so, we wait in hope remembering that "now is the favorable time; behold, now is the day of salvation" (2 Cor. 6:2).

Quiet and Authority

Hoping for the judgment and justice that will come at the return of Christ also reframes our political activity and relationship to worldly authorities. Hope is longed for, not yet possessed. Christian hope doesn't amount to a certain political activism, seeking the achievement of hope's end, but a kind of political quietism that waits expectantly for the revelation of hope with the arrival of the King. Christian mission is not political conquest but proclamation of the coming King and his kingdom.

The mistaken call to political arms has long been a challenge for the church, seen from the early days of Christendom to the enmeshing of the church and political powers through the Middle Ages and the Reformation, to the Kuyperian Dutch experiment, to the contemporary confusion in the United States around religion and political affiliation. Public politics have mistakenly been understood as an advantageous mechanism for bringing the kingdom of God to society. But Christian faith defies the structural boundaries of public politics, eschewing both appeals to the masses and coercive measures to bring transformation, favoring instead the proclamation of the cross over against worldly wisdom (1 Cor. 1:18–31). Where true faith thrives best is not in popular opinion or political power but in the patient hope of eschatological renewal.

The aspiration of the Christian life of hope is a quiet and peaceable existence. This life is contrasted with political agitation. Two of the prominent exhortations to this end in the New Testament are with a view to outsider perception and gospel opportunity. In 1 Thessalonians, addressing an intense environment of persecution, Paul admonishes the church "to aspire to live quietly, and to mind your own affairs, and to work with your hands as we instructed you, so that you may walk properly before outsiders and be dependent on no one" (4:11–12). Believers were not to be aggressive or revolutionaries but honest and hardworking citizens. Their self-sufficiency was intended to be in imitation of Paul's ministry so that no one would mistake financial need as a motivation for gospel proclamation. Instead, by already having what they needed, they could continue proclaiming Christ without any transactional demand. In 1 Timothy, Paul encourages Timothy and the Ephesians to pray for rulers and authorities in society so that the believers "may lead a peaceful and quiet life, godly and dignified in every way" (2:2). This prayer is good and pleasing to God, "who desires all people to be saved and to come to the knowledge of the truth" (2:4). Again, the admonition to peace and quiet is for the purpose of gospel proclamation.[13] Political activism is discouraged in view of creating opportunities for the gospel to be shared.

13. G. K. Beale notes that "living a *quiet life* (*hēsychazō*) either before an unbelieving world or in the presence of an unbelieving mate is seen as one of the crucial ingredients

This sort of peaceable existence in society demands respect for and submission to worldly authorities. Two kingdoms theology builds on the medieval understanding of the two powers—or "swords"—God has ordained for order in his world: the sword of government to rule the common kingdom (society) and the sword of the Lord (wielded by gospel ministers) to rule the redemptive kingdom (church).[14] VanDrunen notes that Reformed theology, especially following Francis Turretin, takes this doctrine in a more christological direction, seeing Christ as the explicit ruler of both domains, disentangling the church and state authorities and the ensuing battle for power between them. Anyone may hold positions of power in the world, including Christians, but this power is restricted to common affairs of temporal significance. Only qualified believers may hold office in the church, with responsibility for the spiritual estate of the people of God.[15]

Within the power structures of the world, Christians are commanded to submit to authorities. The apostle Paul modeled this submission throughout his gospel mission, using the systems of government in God's providence for evangelistic opportunity (cf. Acts 21–28; Phil. 1:12–18). Paul instructs Christians to recognize civil authorities as ministers of God, not over spiritual affairs, but empowered with the moral responsibility of executing temporal justice (Rom. 13:1–7). Likewise, the apostle Peter charges believers to be subject to every authority at each level of civil government, recognizing public living as an opportunity to agree with good order and

influencing non-Christians to come to the faith." *1–2 Thessalonians*, IVP NTCS (IVP Academic, 2003), 126.

14. The two powers originated with Pope Gelasius in the late fifth century, while the two swords came in the early fourteenth century from Pope Boniface VIII in his *Unam Sanctum*. VanDrunen, *Politics After Christendom*, 37–44.

15. I have written elsewhere about the relationship between power domains and the leadership of the church. Chase R. Kuhn, "The Priesthood of All Believers: No Mediator but Christ; a 'New' Shape to Ministry," in *Celebrating the Reformation: Its Legacy and Continuing Relevance*, ed. Mark D. Thompson, Colin Bale, and Edward Loane (Apollos, 2017).

thereby be models of morality (1 Pet. 2:13–17). In giving respect to civil authority, Christians recognize the significance of temporal government in God's common provision, upholding a stage on which the gospel may advance. The greater the civic peace, the better the opportunity for the gospel to spread effectively and with power. Subversion of civic government leads to political tension that may prove prohibitive to gospel mission.

Hope in a political domain, then, means resistance not in the form of political upheaval but of public quiet. Christians demonstrate a higher allegiance to a greater kingdom when they resist the urge to compete for power like the world. Instead, following Christ, they submit to authorities, even at great personal expense, in order to serve and live to righteousness.

Renewal and Transformation

If Christian public engagement is intended to be quiet, with a view to proclamation and witness, what is to be said of cultural participation in this age? H. Richard Niebuhr wisely notes, "It is helpful to remember that the question of Christianity and civilization is by no means a new one; that Christian perplexity in this area has been perennial, and the problem has been an enduring one through all the Christian centuries."[16] At the heart of Niebuhr's iconic book *Christ and Culture*, he identifies culture as something social whereby humans are "concerned with the temporal and material realization of values." Therefore, culture itself carries an inherent sense of morality—seeking good ends. Niebuhr explains, "This does not mean that the goods that human effort seeks to realize are necessarily temporal or material, however much the concern for these is part of cultural achievement."[17] Christians feel an eschatological tension in

16. H. Richard Niebuhr, *Christ and Culture* (Harper & Brothers, 1951), 2.
17. Niebuhr, *Christ and Culture*, 36.

relation to culture. They belong to a subculture of God's people, but they also participate in the society around them. When they have values they hold dear, how will these be—and should they be—realized in the wider world?

In the past few decades, questions of cultural significance have focused especially on work.[18] The value of work is framed in relation to the coming kingdom of God. Frequently, cultural activities (e.g., work) are seen as serving transformational purposes, giving eternal importance to human labor. A prominent proponent of this belief is N. T. Wright, who contends from 1 Corinthians 15:58 that "what you do in the Lord *is not in vain*. . . . God's recreation of his wonderful world, which began with the resurrection of Jesus and continues mysteriously as God's people live in the risen Christ and the power of his Spirit, means that what we do in Christ and by the Spirit in the present is not wasted. It will last all the way into God's new world."[19] Likewise, eschewing the popular notion of a heaven being a purely spiritual, immaterial destination, J. Richard Middleton contends that otherworldly visions of the future owe more to unbiblical sacred/secular dualism than to scriptural witness. Instead, he says, "The good news of the kingdom is nothing less than the healing (literally, the establishing) of the world (*tikkûn ʾôlām*), in which we are all invited to participate."[20] Wright and Middleton aim to correct the long-standing emphasis on escaping the world, which is integral to gospel proclamation in many Christian circles. They note, rightly, that there is a continuity between this world and the

18. David VanDrunen shows how differing theologies—emerging church, contemporary Neo-Calvinism, and the New Perspective on Paul—intersect with one another on the transformational significance of work. *Living in God's Two Kingdoms: A Biblical Vision for Christianity and Culture* (Crossway, 2010), 16–24.

19. N. T. Wright, *Surprised by Hope: Rethinking Heaven, the Resurrection, and the Mission of the Church* (HarperOne, 2008), 208–9.

20. J. Richard Middleton, *A New Heaven and a New Earth: Reclaiming Biblical Eschatology* (Baker Academic, 2014), 262.

eschatological new heavens and new earth, seen historically in the resurrection of Jesus in a human body. But I fear their correction is an overcorrection.[21]

The labor of humanity, redeemed or otherwise, is not intended to build a culture or cultural artifacts for the future earth. In a double effort to recognize a material future *and* extend meaning to more than gospel proclamation, modern theological treatments of work and eschatology have lost sight of one important fact: The new creation is the work of Christ alone. The new creation will certainly be material, as the work of redemption is re-creation, not creation de novo. So, contemporary scholarship is correct in noting that the future will not be otherworldly and that this world will be renewed. However, the attempt to locate the significance of our work in its permanence is misguided. These recent treatments have found worth in endurance; if something matters, it will matter for the kingdom and find a place in the eschatological future.[22] Once more, this thinking is a correction to the belief that the only thing that matters is the soul, and therefore, the only thing of lasting worth is evangelism, as everything else will burn.

A better alternative is to recognize work as good simply because it is part of God's design for the common provision of his world. What makes work distinctively Christian is not its endurance or evangelistic opportunity but the One unto whom the work is done. The apostle Paul urges believers, "Whatever you do, work heartily, as for the Lord and not men" (Col. 3:23). This charge is built on the eschatological hope of an inheritance—where our real "reward" lies (3:24)—and in

21. For more caution against this overcorrection, see Michael Allen, *Grounded in Heaven: Recentering Christian Hope and Life on God* (Eerdmans, 2018). For a clear guide on interpreting 1 Cor. 15:58, see Peter Orr, "Abounding in the Work of the Lord (1 Cor. 15:58): Everything We Do as Christians or Specific Gospel Work?," *Themelios* 38, no. 2 (2013): 205–14.

22. Wright extends this to gardening, machinery, art, music, and good deeds. *Surprised by Hope*, 208.

the assurance of justice—where even our mistreatment will be held to account (3:25).[23]

To push the point a little further, note how our eschatological hope affects our expectations of transformation. The kingdom of God comes to the world through the proclamation of Christ. In this age, in which the kingdom has been inaugurated, disciples of Jesus experience spiritual renewal while awaiting the total (including physical) renewal of the earth at the consummation of the kingdom. Until then, proclamation remains the mission of Christ's followers. However, this mission does not mitigate the moral demands on disciples. Their spiritual renewal demands and empowers moral transformation, which undoubtedly will amount to a positive social impact. But this impact will have no lasting transformational effect on the earth, for this is not the design of our renewal. Rather, the meaning of our morality is living unto the proper end of the earth, the coming of Jesus Christ. In this way, we will testify to the One who brings newness, both now in our lives and fully in the future. Our work as Christians finds its value as we labor with our ultimate end in view. And for those nonbelievers who do not appreciate or appropriate their work unto its ultimate end, their work can still be meaningful as part of God's providence for the world.[24]

Webster notes how this telos frames moral action in appropriate tension, relativizing and inciting action: "It relativizes action, because the end of history is the manifestation of Jesus Christ, the one who was and is and is to come; the end of history is not within the sphere of human competence or responsibility, and is hence a matter of prayer. But it incites action, because the Christian's prayer

23. I have noted accountability as an encouragement to those under others in positions of authority, but the apostle also uses the reality of just judgment as a warning to Christian masters serving in positions of authority over others (Col. 4:1).

24. To be clear, not all work is good. All unbelieving work may be penultimately good, but not necessarily so. There are some categories of work that will always be evil (e.g., exploitation of the vulnerable, theft, etc.).

Maranatha! is an active, not an inactive prayer, a prayer which invites, expects, indeed, commands us to do in our sphere what is fitting in the light of the action of God to whom we pray."[25] What is the action that accords with prayerful expectation? It is the active trust in the work of Christ—work that is powerful over sin in our lives, even now; work that is powerful enough to transform the cosmos and liberate it from the grip of sin's curse in the coming day; work that will be known fully on that last day when all social injustices will be judged; work that is powerful enough to "finish" that which has already begun. When we attempt the work of cultural transformation, we inadvertently take the place of Christ, the sole Redeemer and hope of the world.[26]

Hope leads to waiting. It is the expectation of the fulfillment of God's promises. And it is precisely this expectation that leads to a form of action. "Beloved, we are God's children now, and what we will be has not yet appeared; but we know that when he appears we shall be like him, because we shall see him as he is. And everyone who thus hopes in him purifies himself as he is pure" (1 John 3:2–3). Our hope as the children of God rests in the love of God. As we wait, we grow in love anticipating the revelation of Christ, that beatific vision, when we will see God.

Love

The mode of living by faith in hope is love. Indeed, love is supreme. Faith will become sight. Hope will be realized. But "love never ends"

25. Webster, "Eschatology and Anthropology," 284–85.

26. As we saw in chap. 5, the fulfillment of the world's telos belongs to Jesus alone. Thus, I agree with VanDrunen, "The kingdom of God proclaimed by the Lord Jesus Christ is *not* built through politics, commerce, music, or sports. Redemption does not consist in restoring people to fulfill Adam's original task, but consists in the Lord Jesus himself fulfilling Adam's original task once and for all, on our behalf. Thus redemption is not 'creation regained' but 're-creation gained.'" *Living in God's Two Kingdoms*, 26. VanDrunen's challenge to "creation regained" is an implicit reference to Al Wolters, *Creation Regained: Biblical Basics for a Reformational Worldview*, 2nd ed. (Eerdmans, 2005).

(1 Cor. 13:8). To be certain, faith, hope, and love are *all* required for Christian living in this age. But what faith hopes in is the love of God, which brings everlasting life. In fact, God himself is love, and our life is in Christ. In this concluding section, I hope to demonstrate the endurance of love as the grounds of confidence for moral living in the present age. This life requires ongoing patience, demonstrating love in tangible ways that give expression to God's unseen presence. Love now gives a foretaste of the love to be revealed fully, when the pure in heart will see God (Matt. 5:8).

Endurance and the Perfection of Moral Goodness

Life's journey in faith does not terminate in faith. In fact, because of the hope set before us in God's "precious and very great promises" (2 Pet. 1:4), the apostle Peter exhorts believers to "make every effort to supplement faith" with a host of virtues (1:5–7), chief among them being love.[27] The terminus of the hope given by God is believers becoming "partakers of the divine nature, having escaped from the corruption that is in the world because of sinful desire" (1:4). The notion of participating in the divine nature is known traditionally as *theosis*, or deification. While transformation is part of the sanctification of believers, it is perfected at glorification. Nonetheless, the process is important as it is intimately connected to living in faith. Believers participate in divine love, according to the new life given by the Holy Spirit. As they do so, they are being perfected.

But so long as this love is expressed in this life, entangled in the concerns of the world, it will always be mixed with self-love. Only in the new creation, in resurrection glory, will love be pure and perfect. Believers then will truly and fully know and love God, and all their

27. That love is chief can be seen from where it falls in the sequence of 2 Pet. 1, love being final in the series. But even if this argument is unpersuasive, love as the principal virtue is evident in other texts; cf. Gal. 5:13; Eph. 5:1–2; Col. 3:14.

love for others will be properly ordered in God.[28] Then will our nature share (commune) perfectly with the divine nature, that is to say, "be conformable to God," deified. Turretin describes this union as "nothing else than a certain effusion and emanation (*aporroē*) of the deity upon the souls of the saints, communicating to them the image of all his perfections, as much as they can belong unto a creature."[29] This, John Calvin says, is the end of the gospel.[30]

Waiting for Love

The end of all things serves as motivation and assurance—interconnected realities—of the moral life. Our actions and our way of being will be held to account by God. Every thought, word, and deed springing from our hearts will be judged. Apart from grace, this is terrifying, "for our God is a consuming fire" (Heb. 12:28). But because of God's love—the love that is perfected in us—there is no longer fear of judgment, for "perfect love casts out fear" (1 John 4:17–18). Instead, love motivates love: "We love because he first loved us" (4:19). It is the appreciation of God's great love that both liberates and drives a love for others.

John's first epistle testifies to and proclaims Christ—the Word of life, eternal life—in order that there may be "fellowship" among believers, and with God himself (1 John 1:3). Abiding in truth incorporates believers into a communion of joy and life. They participate even in God. This participation is not ontological, making creatures one in essence with the Godhead, but rather is moral, conforming our nature to the divine. Thus, creatures are allowed into that most holy relationship, delighting in the presence of God. It was to this

28. Francis Turretin, *Institutes of Elenctic Theology*, 3 vols., trans. George Musgrave Giger, ed. James T. Dennison Jr. (P&R, 1994), 3:20.8.15.

29. Turretin, *Institutes of Elenctic Theology*, 3:20.8.15.

30. John Calvin, commentary on 2 Pet. 1:4 in vol. 22 of *Calvin's Commentaries* (Baker, 1981).

end that Jesus committed believers, both his disciples and all who would come after them, that "they may all be one, just as you Father, are in me, and I in you, that they may also be in us" (John 17:21). This participation in intimate relationship is none other than "love" (17:26). While we anticipate the fullness of love that will be known in the beatific vision, we have a foretaste of that vision—giving visibility to the invisible—in our love for one another. "No one has ever seen God; if we love one another, God abides in us and his love is perfected in us" (1 John 4:12).

Beatific Vision

Though we have never seen God, the hope of salvation is that "we will see his face" (Rev. 22:3; cf. Ps. 11:7). This is the genuine telos of humanity, the proper ordering to the triune God in worship. The culmination of salvation history is when God will dwell with his people and finally deliver perfect peace and order to the world. In the Lord's presence, there will no longer be anything accursed, nor any darkness (Rev. 22:3–5). There will be no tears or sorrow, no pain or death because the things of old—the cursed things—will have gone (21:4). The Lord himself will make all things new, showing himself to be the first and the last (21:5–6). In other words, morality and ethics will cease; the world will be perfectly good.

This beatific vision is, in one sense, impossible. God cannot be seen (Exod. 33:20). And yet "we do well to speak . . . of the visibility of the invisible God."[31] The wonder of God's grace, which accommodates us in our creaturely finitude and moral need, is that the Son of God took on flesh. In the Lord Jesus, we have seen God (John 1:18; cf. 14:6–10). In the face of the Lord Jesus, we will behold God. When we do, it will be seen, fully and finally, what God has planned since before the foundation of the world—that in Christ, all things are

31. Allen, *Grounded in Heaven*, 83.

brought together (Eph. 1:10).[32] God is good, and his plans for the world are good. The future for those who are found in the Son is the perfection of goodness and the realization of our final happiness.[33] When we see God, we will see the end of ethics.

32. The Greek word *anakephalaiomai* is rendered in the ESV as "unite," but other possible renderings are, as I've indicated, "bring together" or "sum up." "Recapitulate" is another option, though BDAG does not give preference to this rendering in Eph. 1. If the word is rendered in Eph. 1 this way, which is possible, it would demonstrate that Christ is the focal point of history. This is certainly fitting and agreeable with the grand vision of salvation history.

33. Augustine, *The City of God* 19.4 (*NPNF*[1] 2:401–3).

Acknowledgments

Work on this book began ten years ago when I was told I would be teaching ethics alongside other theology units at Moore College. I was daunted by the task, not only by the sheer challenge of such a unit of study, but also by the history of those who had ably gone before me. When I was a seminary student, I didn't value ethics as much as I should have, viewing it as only tangential to my love of systematic theology. Years later, after further study and serving as a pastor, I knew what I should have recognized long before: Ethics is integral to theology. I was convinced that I needed to persuade students that our beliefs about God and the gospel are not abstract but profoundly affect our daily lives. I express my gratitude to Mark Thompson (Principal, Moore College) for pushing me to embark on the adventure of teaching ethics as a theologian. I am also grateful for the fellowship with colleagues at Moore College and the many stimulating conversations around the office, over morning tea, and at faculty lunches that have formed me. In particular, it is worth naming those in the Theology, Philosophy, and Ethics Department: Andrew Leslie, Mark Earngey, and David Höhne.

I spent concentrated time writing this book over two sabbaticals (2019, 2023) generously afforded me by the Governing Board of Moore College. I am grateful for this leave. I am especially thankful for the support of the board when, during the conclusion of my last sabbatical, I was called back to parish ministry. The board and the principal value the work of the college in service of the local church, and I am grateful for their demonstration of this in their releasing me to return to the pastorate.

During my sabbaticals, I was shown generous hospitality. In 2019, William and Janet Taylor kindly allowed my family and me to stay in London for a month. Simon and Rebecca Pillar, with their children, welcomed us to stay in Oxford for four months during the Michaelmas term. During that time, Wycliffe Hall provided me with meals and access to the Bodleian Libraries, and welcomed me into their college fellowship as a visiting scholar. Andrew Atherstone was the kind facilitator of this privilege, and I am grateful for his friendship and partnership in the gospel. While in Oxford, St. Ebbe's was a wonderful church home for us, and Emmanuel Christian School was a welcoming learning community for my children. My second sabbatical was undertaken at home in Sydney, but I was shown hospitality nonetheless. Barbara Stephens kindly welcomed me and two colleagues to stay at her farm in Jamberoo, New South Wales, for a weeklong writing retreat. The time afforded us for work and fellowship was invaluable.

Many friends have supported me and discussed ideas or read bits along the way, including Jane Tooher, Dan Wu, Philip Kern, Grant Taylor, Tony Payne, Karen Beilharz, Andrew Errington, Matthew Cunningham, and Serena Eveleigh. Elliot Ritzema played a crucial role in the first draft of this book, offering many suggestions for improvement. I'm also thankful for "The Breakfast Club" with Peter Orr, Paul Grimmond, and Simon Gillham that met most Friday mornings for prayer and mutual encouragement.

I've benefited from presenting several drafts of chapters at various conferences and receiving peer feedback. These include the Theology Connect conference (2018, Sydney), the Moore College faculty conference (2020, Sydney), the Australia New Zealand Association of Theological Studies (ANZATS) conference (2021, online), the Reformed Forum Symposium on Reformed Moral Theology (2023, online), the Trinity Theological College Annual Lecture (2023, Perth), and numerous talks through the Centre for Christian Living at Moore College (2019–2023).

More than conferences, the most helpful testing ground for this material has been the classroom, from undergraduate classes to graduate seminars. Students have patiently endured the formulation of this material over many years, raising many searching questions and providing me with enriching conversations.

It is worth noting that two scholars have significantly impacted my thinking about theological ethics. The first is Oliver O'Donovan, whom I've never met but whose work I have admired from a distance for years. I've appreciated the depth of insights and the freshness with which his writing has challenged and stimulated my thinking. He was the first to help me see how Christ gives us confidence in the moral order. The second is David VanDrunen, who has become a friend. Dave's thinking has helped me piece together several theological puzzles, particularly around natural law. I am grateful for the example Dave has set me (and many others) of a deep commitment to the Scriptures, academic rigor, clarity in writing style, and humble and generous engagement with others.

I'm grateful for the privilege of publishing with Baker Books. Thanks especially to Amy Nemecek and Eddie LaRow for your professionalism and care in preparing the manuscript for publication and to Sarah Gordon for the cover design.

Finally, my family have continued to be a wonderful support to me. Amy, my wife, has supported and encouraged me in my work, directly and indirectly, serving as the most wonderful partner in ministry. My children have been a great source of joy, grounding me at the end of a long day of contemplation and getting lost in books. As much as anything, my children—Olive, Ezra, Penelope, and Marigold—were my motivation for this book. I want them to grow up confident that there is a moral order. God is good, he has made the world good, and we can know ultimate goodness through his Son, Jesus. It is to my children that I dedicate this book.

Bibliography

Adams, Robert Merrihew. *Finite and Infinite Goods: A Framework for Ethics*. Oxford University Press, 1999.

Allen, Michael. *Grounded in Heaven: Recentering the Christian Hope and Life on God*. Eerdmans, 2018.

Anselm of Canterbury. *Monologion*. In *The Major Works: Including Monologion, Proslogion, and Why God Became Man*. Oxford World's Classics. Oxford University Press, 1998.

Aquinas, Thomas. *Summa Contra Gentiles, Book Two: Creation*. Translated by James F. Anderson. University of Notre Dame Press, 1956.

———. *Summa Theologica*. 5 vols. Christian Classics, 1948.

Aristotle. *Nicomachean Ethics*. Edited by Lesley Brown. Translated by David Ross. Oxford's World's Classics. Oxford University Press, 2009.

Augustine. *The Problem of Free Choice* (*De Libero Arbitrio*). In vol. 22 of Ancient Christian Writers. Translated and annotated by Dom Mark Pontifex. Longman, Greens and Co., 1955.

Barth, Karl. *Church Dogmatics*. 14 vols. Edited by G. W. Bromiley and T. F. Torrance. Hendrickson, 2004.

———. *Dogmatics in Outline*. Harper & Row, 1959.

———. *Ethics*. Edited by Dietrich Braun. Translated by Geoffrey W. Bromiley. Wipf & Stock, 1981.

Bavinck, Herman. *Christian Worldview*. Edited and translated by Nathaniel Gray Sutanto, James Eglinton, and Cory C. Brock. Crossway, 2019.

———. *Reformed Dogmatics*. Vol. 2, *God and Creation*. Edited by John Bolt. Translated by John Vriend. Baker Academic, 2004.

Beale, G. K. *1–2 Thessalonians*. IVP NTCS. IVP Academic, 2003.

Black, Rufus. *Christian Moral Realism: Natural Law, Narrative, Virtue, and the Gospel*. Oxford University Press, 2000.

Bonhoeffer, Dietrich. *Creation and Fall: A Theological Interpretation of Genesis 1–3*. Macmillan, 1959.

———. *Ethics*. Vol. 6 of DBW. Edited by Clifford J. Green. Translated by Reinhard Krauss, Charles C. West, and Douglas W. Stott. Fortress, 2005.

———. *Life Together and Prayerbook of the Bible*. Vol. 5 of DBW. Edited by Geffrey B. Kelly. Translated by Daniel W. Bloesch and James H. Burtness. Fortress, 1996.

Bray, Gerald. "The Significance of God's Image in Man." *Tyndale Bulletin* 42, no. 2 (1991): 195–225.

Brock, Brian. *Singing the Ethos of God: On the Place of Christian Ethics in Scripture*. Eerdmans, 2005.

Brunner, Emil. *The Divine Imperative: A Study in Christian Ethics*. Translated by Olive Wyon. Lutterworth, 1964.

Bullinger, Heinrich. *The Decades of Henry Bullinger*. 2 vols. Edited by Thomas Harding. Reformation Heritage, 2004.

Calvin, John. *Institutes of the Christian Religion*. 2 vols. Edited by John T. McNeill. Translated by Ford Lewis Battles. Westminster, 1960.

———. *Calvin's Commentaries*. 22 vols. Baker, 1981.

Chappell, Timothy. "Euthyphro's 'Dilemma,' Socrates' *Daimonion* and Plato's God." In *God, Goodness and Philosophy*. Edited by Harriet A. Harris. Ashgate, 2011.

Dryden, J. de Waal. *A Hermeneutic of Wisdom: Recovering the Formative Agency of Scripture*. Baker Academic, 2018.

Dumbrell, William. *The Search for Order: Biblical Eschatology in Focus*. Baker, 1994.

Edwards, Jonathan. *The Religious Affections*. Banner of Truth, 1961/2007.

———. *The Works of Jonathan Edwards*. 2 vols. Revised by Edward Hickman. Banner of Truth, 1974.

Errington, Andrew. *Every Good Path: Wisdom and Practical Reason in Christian Ethics and the Book of Proverbs*. T&T Clark, 2020.

———. "Forgiveness and the Novelty of Christian Ethics," *Modern Theology* 39, no. 3 (July 2023): 472–89.

Forrester, Duncan. *On Human Worth*. SCM, 2001.

Gericke, Jaco. "Beyond Divine Command Theory: Moral Realism in the Hebrew Bible." In *God, Goodness and Philosophy*. Edited by Harriet A. Harris. Ashgate, 2011.

Grabill, Stephen J. *Rediscovering the Natural Law in Reformed Theological Ethics*. Eerdmans, 2006.

Gunton, Colin. *The Triune Creator: A Historical and Systematic Study*. Eerdmans, 1998.

Hare, John E. *God's Call: Moral Realism, God's Commands, and Human Autonomy*. Eerdmans, 2001.

Harrison, Glynn. *A Better Story: God, Sex, and Human Flourishing*. Inter-Varsity, 2016.

Hauerwas, Stanley. *A Community of Character: Toward a Constructive Christian Social Ethic*. University of Notre Dame Press, 1981.

———. *The Peaceable Kingdom: A Primer in Christian Ethics*. 2nd ed. SCM, 2003.

Helm, Paul. *Reforming Free Will: A Conversation on the History of Reformed Views on Compatibilism (1500–1800)*. Mentor, 2020.

Hoekema, Anthony A. *Created in God's Image*. Eerdmans, 1986.

Hooker, Richard. *The Laws of Ecclesiastical Polity in Modern English*. Edited by Bradford Littlejohn, Bradley Belschner, and Brian Marr, with Sean Duncan. Davenant Press, 2019.

Horton, Michael. *The Christian Faith: A Systematic Theology for Pilgrims on the Way*. Zondervan Academic, 2011.

———. *Lord and Servant: A Covenant Christology*. Westminster John Knox, 2005.

———. *Rediscovering the Holy Spirit: God's Perfecting Presence in Creation, Redemption, and Everyday Life*. Zondervan Academic, 2017.

Hume, David. *A Treatise on Human Nature*. Edited by David Fate Norton and Mary J. Norton. Oxford University Press, 2000.

Hunsinger, George. "*Salvator Mundi*: Three Types of Christology." In *Christology, Ancient and Modern: Explorations in Constructive Dogmatics*. Edited by Oliver D. Crisp and Fred Sanders. Zondervan, 2013.

Kant, Immanuel. *Groundwork of the Metaphysics of Morals*. Rev. ed. Translated and edited by Mary Gregor and Jens Timmermann. Cambridge University Press, 2012.

Kapic, Kelly M. "Anthropology." In *Christian Dogmatics: Reformed Theology for the Church Catholic*. Edited by Michael Allen and Scott R. Swain. Baker Academic, 2016.

Kelsey, David H. *Eccentric Existence: A Theological Anthropology*. 2 vols. Westminster John Knox, 2009.

Kierkegaard, Søren. *Fear and Trembling: Dialectical Lyric by Johannes de Silentio*. Translated by Alastair Hannay. Penguin, 1985.

Kilner, John F. *Dignity and Destiny: Humanity in the Image of God*. Eerdmans, 2015.

Kline, Meredith G. *Genesis: A New Commentary*. Edited by Jonathan G. Kline. Hendrickson, 2016.

———. *Kingdom Prologue: Genesis Foundations for a Covenantal Worldview*. Two Age Press, 2000.

Kraal, Anders. "Does Divine Simplicity Solve the Euthyphro Dilemma?" In *God, Goodness and Philosophy*. Edited by Harriet A. Harris. Ashgate, 2011.

Kuhn, Chase R. "The Doctrine of the Church and Age-Specific Ministries." In *Australian Evangelical Perspectives on Youth Ministry: Identity, Church, Culture, and Discipleship*. Edited by Ruth Lukabyo. Wipf & Stock, 2023.

———. *The Ecclesiology of Donald Robinson and D. Broughton Knox: Exposition, Analysis, and Theological Evaluation*. Wipf & Stock, 2017.

———. "Figural Reading Within Contemporary Theological Interpretation of Scripture: Problems and Parameters." In *Revelation and Reason in Christian Theology*. Edited by David I. Starling and Christopher C. Green. Lexham Press, 2018.

———. "In Defence of the 'Big Idea': Key Questions for Faithful Preaching." In *Preacher, Pastor and Evangelist: Essays on the Work of Ministry, in Honour of Simon Manchester*. Edited by Gerard O'Brien. Matthias Media, 2019.

———. "The Priesthood of All Believers: No Mediator but Christ; A 'New' Shape to Ministry." In *Celebrating the Reformation: Its Legacy and Continuing Relevance*. Edited by Mark D. Thompson, Colin Bale, and Edward Loane. Apollos, 2017.

———. "Theology for Preaching, Preaching for Theology." In *Theology Is for Preaching: Biblical Foundations, Method, and Practice*. Edited by Chase R. Kuhn and Paul Grimmond. Lexham Press, 2021.

Leith, Edward. *Treatise of Divinity Consisting of Three Books*. London, 1646.

Levering, Matthew. *Engaging the Doctrine of Creation: Cosmos, Creatures, and the Wise and Good Creator*. Baker Academic, 2017.

Luther, Martin. *The Keys*. In vol. 40 of *Luther's Works*. Edited by Conrad Bergendoff. Translated by Helmut T. Lehmann. Fortress, 1958.

MacIntyre, Alasdair. *After Virtue: A Study in Moral Theory*. 3rd ed. University of Notre Dame Press, 2007.

Mastricht, Petrus van. *Faith in the Triune God*. Vol. 2 of *Theoretical-Practical Theology*. Edited by Joel R. Beeke. Translated by Todd M. Rester. Reformation Heritage, 2019.

———. *The Works of God and the Fall of Man*. Vol. 3 of *Theoretical-Practical Theology*. Edited by Joel R. Beeke. Translated by Todd M. Rester. Reformation Heritage, 2021.

Matthews, Kenneth A. *Genesis 1–11:26*. New American Commentary Series. Broadman & Holman, 1996.

Middleton, J. Richard. *The Liberating Image: The* Imago Dei *in Genesis 1*. Brazos, 2005.

———. *A New Heaven and a New Earth: Reclaiming Biblical Eschatology*. Baker Academic, 2014.

Muller, Richard. *Divine Will and Human Choice*. Baker Academic, 2017.

Murray, John. *Principles of Conduct: Aspects of Biblical Ethics*. Eerdmans, 1957.

Niebuhr, H. Richard. *Christ and Culture*. Harper & Brothers, 1951.

Niebuhr, Reinhold. *The Nature and Destiny of Man: A Christian Interpretation*. One-volume ed. Scribner's Sons, 1949.

Nietzsche, Friedrich. *Beyond Good and Evil*. Translated by Marion Faber. Oxford University Press, 1998.

Nouwen, Henri J. M. *In the Name of Jesus: Reflections on Christian Leadership*. Crossroad, 1989.

O'Donovan, Oliver. *Common Objects of Love: Moral Reflection on the Shaping of Community*. Eerdmans, 2002.

———. *The Desire of the Nations: Rediscovering the Roots of Political Theology*. Cambridge University Press, 1996.

———. *Resurrection and Moral Order: An Outline for Evangelical Ethics*. 2nd ed. Apollos, 1994.

———. *Self, World, and Time*. Vol. 1 of *Ethics as Theology*. Eerdmans, 2013.

———. *The Ways of Judgment*. Eerdmans, 2005.

———. "What Can Ethics Know About God?" In *The Doctrine of God and Theological Ethics*. Edited by Alan J. Torrance and Michael Banner. T&T Clark, 2006.

Orr, Peter. "Abounding in the Work of the Lord (1 Cor. 15:58): Everything We Do as Christians or Specific Gospel Work?" *Themelios* 38, no. 2 (2013): 205–14.

Pannenberg, Wolfhart. *Ethics*. Translated by Keith Crim. Westminster, 1981.

———. *Systematic Theology*. 3 vols. Eerdmans, 1991.

Plato. *Euthyphro*. Vol. 1 of *Plato in Twelve Volumes*. Translated by Harold North Fowler. Harvard University Press, 1966.

Quinn, Philip L. "Theological Voluntarism." In *The Oxford Handbook of Ethical Theory*. Edited by David Copp. Oxford University Press, 2006.

Reno, R. R. *Genesis*. BTCB. Brazos, 2010.

Ross, Allen P. *Creation and Blessing: A Guide to the Study and Exposition of Genesis*. Baker, 1998.

Sayers, Dorothy. "The Other Six Deadly Sins." In *Letters to a Diminished Church: Passionate Arguments for the Relevance of Christian Doctrine*. Thomas Nelson, 2004.

Schwöbel, Christoph. "God, Creation, and the Christian Community: The Dogmatic Basis of a Creation Ethic of Createdness." In *The Doctrine of Creation: Essays in Dogmatics, History and Philosophy*. Edited by Colin E. Gunton. T&T Clark, 1997.

———. "Recovering Human Dignity." In *God and Human Dignity*. Edited by R. Kendall Soulen and Linda Woodhead. Eerdmans, 2006.

———. "We Are All God's Vocabulary: The Idea of Creation as a Speech-Act of the Trinitarian God and Its Significance for the Dialogue Between Theology and Sciences." In vol. 1 of *Knowing Creation: Perspectives from Theology, Philosophy, and Science*. Edited by Andrew B. Torrance and Thomas H. McCall. Zondervan Academic, 2018.

Smith, James K. A. "Reforming Public Theology: Two Kingdoms, or Two Cities?" *Calvin Theological Journal* 47 (2012): 122–37.

Smith, Robert S. "Cultural Marxism: Imaginary Conspiracy or Revolutionary Reality?" *Themelios* 44, no. 3 (2019): 436–65.

Starling, David I. *Hermeneutics as Apprenticeship: How the Bible Shapes Our Interpretive Habits and Practices*. Baker Academic, 2016.

Strange, Dan. "Not Ashamed! The Sufficiency of Scripture for Public Theology." *Themelios* 36, no. 2 (2011): 238–60.

Taylor, Charles. *The Ethics of Authenticity*. Harvard University Press, 1992.

———. *Sources of the Self: The Making of Modern Identity*. Harvard University Press, 1988.

Thielman, Frank. *Ephesians*. BECNT. Baker Academic, 2010.

———. *Romans*. ZECNT. Zondervan, 2018.

Torrance, Thomas F. *Atonement: The Person and Work of Christ*. Edited by Robert T. Walker. IVP Academic, 2009.

———. *Incarnation: The Person and Life of Christ*. Edited by Robert T. Walker. IVP Academic, 2008.

———. *Space, Time and Resurrection*. T&T Clark, 2019.

Trueman, Carl R. *The Rise and Triumph of the Modern Self: Cultural Amnesia, Expressive Individualism, and the Road to Sexual Revolution*. Crossway, 2020.

———. "The Strange Fate of *Hamilton* and *Harry Potter*." *First Things*, January 6, 2022. https://www.firstthings.com/web-exclusives/2022/01/the-strange-fate-of-hamilton-and-harry-potter.

Turretin, Francis. *Institutes of Elenctic Theology*. 3 vols. Translated by George Musgrave Giger. Edited by James T. Dennison Jr. P&R, 1994.

VanDrunen, David. *Divine Covenants and Moral Order: A Biblical Theology of Natural Law*. Eerdmans, 2014.

———. "The Importance of the Penultimate: Reformed Social Thought and the Contemporary Critiques of the Liberal Society." *Journal of Markets & Morality* 9, no. 2 (Fall 2006): 219–49.

———. *Living in God's Two Kingdoms: A Biblical Vision for Christianity and Culture*. Crossway, 2010.

———. *Natural Law: A Short Companion*. Essentials in Christian Ethics. B&H Academic, 2023.

———. *Natural Law and the Two Kingdoms: A Study in the Development of Reformed Social Thought*. Eerdmans, 2010.

———. *Politics After Christendom: Political Theology in a Fractured World.* Zondervan Academic, 2020.

Vanhoozer, Kevin J. *The Drama of Doctrine: A Canonical-Linguistic Approach to Christian Theology*. Westminster John Knox, 2005.

———. *Is There a Meaning in This Text? The Bible, the Reader, and the Morality of Literary Knowledge*. Zondervan, 1998.

Vermigli, Peter Martyr. *On Free Will and the Law*. Vol. 2 of *A New Translation of the Loci Communes (1576).* Translated and edited by Joseph A. Tipton. Davenant Press, 2021.

———. *On Original Sin*. Vol. 1 of *A New Translation of the Loci Communes (1576).* Translated and edited by Kirk Summers. Davenant Press, 2019.

Vos, Geerhardus. *Biblical Theology: Old and New Testaments*. Banner of Truth, 1975.

———. *The Eschatology of the Old Testament*. Edited by James T. Dennison Jr. P&R, 2001.

Watson, Thomas. *All Things for Good.* Banner of Truth, 1986.

Webster, John. *God Without Measure: Working Papers in Christian Theology*. 2 vols. T&T Clark, 2015.

———. *Word and Church: Essays in Christian Dogmatics*. T&T Clark, 2001.

Whitehead, Colson. "How 'You Do You' Perfectly Captures Our Narcissistic Culture." *New York Times*, March 31, 2015. https://www.nytimes.com/2015/04/05/magazine/how-you-do-you-perfectly-captures-our-narcissistic-culture.html.

Wolters, Albert M. *Creation Regained: Biblical Basics for a Reformational Worldview*. 2nd ed. Eerdmans, 2005.

Wright, N. T. *Surprised by Hope: Rethinking Heaven, the Resurrection, and the Mission of the Church*. Harper One, 2008.

Yoder, John Howard. *The Original Revolution*. Herald, 1971.

Scripture Index

Subject Index

Chase R. Kuhn serves as rector of St Matthias Anglican Church, Centennial Park. Previously, he served as lecturer in theology and ethics and director of the Centre for Christian Living at Moore Theological College, Sydney. He has authored, edited, and contributed to several other books focused on the application of theology.